ANGLO-AMERICAN
RELATIONS
1861–1865

BY

BROUGHAM VILLIERS

AND

W. H. CHESSON

KENNIKAT PRESS
Port Washington, N. Y./London

327.42073
S534a

ANGLO-AMERICAN RELATIONS

First published in 1919
Reissued in 1972 by Kennikat Press
Library of Congress Catalog Card No: 70-159714
ISBN 0-8046-1673-6

Manufactured by Taylor Publishing Company   Dallas, Texas

ANGLO-AMERICAN RELATIONS
1861–1865

PREFACE

THE importance to the world of the continuation and extension of the good feeling now happily prevailing between the two great English-speaking peoples is so generally recognised that a clear account of the manner in which, at an important crisis in history, the relations between the sister nations became strained and almost hostile, may not be without its uses. Mutual good will must be based on mutual understanding, and it is unfortunately very easy for misunderstandings to arise even between peoples who enjoy the advantage of a common language. This was the case during the American Civil War, as the records on which we have based this work abundantly show.

We acknowledge, with thanks, services courteously rendered by Miss Julia Eastwood Chesson in searching newspapers, and Mr. Arthur B. Potter in permitting the publication of some interesting anecdotes. To Mr. Fisher Unwin we are indebted for the loan of material relevant to our subject, and we may remark that it is appropriate that our publisher should be one who worked on the Executive Committee of the Anglo-American League of 1898–1903.

We both wish that it had been possible to say more about the men and women of worth who laboured in the cause. Besides the people mentioned in our text, the Vice-presidents of the Union and Emancipation Society included, amongst others : Thomas Bazley, M.P., Guildford J. H. Onslow, M.P., Duncan M'Laren, M.P., Lieut.-General T. Perronet Thompson, Professor Rolleston, Professor Henry J. Stephen Smith, the Rev. Thomas Guthrie, D.D., the Rev. Samuel Davidson, LL.D., the Rev. J. Parker, D.D., the Rev. C. M. Birrell, the Rev. Robert R. Drummond, Charles Sturge, John Epps, Jacob Bright, and Samuel Pope.

B. V.
W. H. C.

CONTENTS

ANGLO-AMERICAN RELATIONS

CHAPTER I

INTRODUCTORY

THE storm that broke over Europe in 1914 wrecked with many others one project of peculiar interest to the various nations which now speak the English tongue. In the year 1915 occurred the centenary of the Treaty of Ghent, which brought to an end an unhappy war between this country and the United States of America, and powerful committees had been formed in both countries to celebrate in a fitting manner the hundred years of peace between the sister nations that had followed that event. The full history of the relations between them during that period would be an instructive study to the statesman anxious to learn what to do and what to avoid in international politics.

Generally, to the present writer at least, it appears largely a record of unwise even mischievous speaking and thinking, but on the whole of rational and honourable doing; of two peoples vehemently conscious of each other's shortcomings, and never very guarded in the expression of their disapproval or resentment, yet fundamentally so very much at one in their outlook and ideas, that though only perhaps towards the close of the period they attained to cordiality, yet they never actually came to strife. Between the United States and ourselves have been waged some of the most reckless and offensive verbal battles in history; while the same nations, as soon as they have come to grips with any question, have repeatedly come to a fair-minded and sensible agreement on the subject, and have afterwards kept it with an invariable loyalty worthy of all praise. Of the differences between the English-speaking peoples it may fairly be said that as long as they are half understood they produce the maximum of friction; as soon as they are fully understood they produce no difficulty at all.

Till the year 1817 each nation had quite a formidable fleet on the great lakes, consisting of thirty or forty vessels of various sizes, mounting in all several hundreds of guns. But by a friendly agreement made in that year the rival Powers covenanted to reduce these armaments to two gunboats, each mounting one gun only, to act as revenue cutters. This scale of armament has never been exceeded since, and no attempt has ever been made, even in times of imminent stress and ill-feeling, to violate the admirable treaty so quietly arranged in 1817.

In the period 1840 to 1850 were quietly settled two vexed questions of boundary between the States and Canada, that between the Province of New Brunswick and Maine in 1842 and that of the western district in 1846. This latter settlement, indeed, followed a violent agitation in the States in which an active party came into being. Under the watchword of "Forty-three forty or fight" the question was pushed to the front, but was soon settled without bloodshed, and was forgotten almost as quickly as it had arisen.

It may be doubted whether the various questions dealt with and settled between the two great English-speaking nations from the Treaty of 1817 to the General Arbitra-

tion Treaty signed after the commencement
of this war, can be equalled for general
sanity and fairness by any similar number
of agreements made between any other
Powers since history began. Nor, as far as
definite acts are concerned, have the relations between any two nations ever been at
once so intimate and so free from serious
injury to one another. It is impossible, of
course, that in two countries, each inhabited
by many millions of human beings, no high-
handed or unjustifiable thing should be done,
but looking over the history of the hundred
years it seems to me that only one really
serious injury was done by one side to the
other—the building and release by England
of the *Alabama* and other Confederate cruisers,
and the consequent destruction of so large a
part of the American merchant shipping.
Other matter of debate between the two
nations led to high words and to threats, if
not to the danger of war, but it may safely
be said that no one was of such magnitude
as to give any excuse for such a crime.

And yet, until nearly the close of the
period, until, in fact, the outbreak of the
Spanish-American War, it cannot be said
that the relations between Britain and America

were particularly friendly. Americans have been more often enraged against us than against all the other nations of the world put together. We, on our part, have had too many disputes with Continental Powers to allow us to allot to a country so much further off and so obviously unaggressive more than a share in our frequent fits of anti-foreign ill-humour. Our Press, at least, however, has been frequently offensive, minatory and patronising, particularly in the period with which we have to deal.

This curious state of things—a comparatively high level of common sense and fairness in dealing with practical questions, with rather more than the average of unwisdom and even ill-feeling in the preliminary discussion of them—may partly be explained by the history of the two nations. The stock from which both have sprung being the same, there are common to both a large variety of movements, ideas, problems and aspirations, which either do not exist at all or exist in very different forms outside the Anglo-Celtic world. This fact insures that hardly any question agitated in one of the countries can fail more or less to arouse interest in the other. The community of language, of course, greatly strengthens this tendency by making not only the literary masterpieces, but even the current social and political condition of either country more or less known in the other. Yet this knowledge often goes only far enough to render misunderstandings possible, for the geographical and political separation of the two peoples has necessarily modified in most cases the aspect of questions common to both. What is easy to do in England is hard to do in America and *vice versa*, owing to conditions peculiar to one country or the other.

During the colonial period the original thirteen States had been peopled mainly by English colonists, who brought besides a common love of liberty what we may call the " Cavalier " or the " Puritan " attitude towards life and politics. Circumstances had tended, on the whole, to gather together most of those likely to sympathise on any question with the privileged classes in this country in the South, while those with whom the lower and middle classes have had most in common were overwhelmingly preponderant in the Northern States. The community of blood insured two things : first, that in any question strongly interesting

Americans, British people were certainly likely to form and express opinions and to take sides much more freely than any other people in the old world; and, secondly, that they were pretty sure to be divided in their sympathies very much as Americans were divided. This was, in itself, a dangerous state of things. Absolute indifference is the surest guarantee of neutrality, but complete moral indifference to the American quarrel was impossible to Englishmen. On the other hand, the very similarity of the nations rendered it impossible for our people as a whole to render complete sympathy to either side in the Civil War. Yet in the heated atmosphere of war it was inevitable that both sides would look to their relations in the old country for a sympathy which they would hardly expect from people of alien blood and speech. Neither side was likely to meet with the response it expected, and both were certain to resent the want of it. This seems to be exactly what happened. During the war the people of the North were far more angry with us than with the French Emperor, though it is certain that Louis Napoleon was more eager to acknowledge the South than we were, and though at the time he was defying the Monroe doctrine by his Mexican expedition. Yet we were nearly, if not quite, as much disliked by the South, whose agents vainly tried to get us to acknowledge their Government.

The feeling in this country presented a curious analogy to that in the United States themselves. There, while opinion was divided —for how otherwise could there have been a war?—the vast preponderance of opinion was in favour of the Union and against slavery; here, though there was much sympathy with the South on the matter of secession, the nation was practically unanimous against slavery. In both countries it was far easier to mobilise the sympathisers with reaction than the friends of freedom and union; and just as in the earlier days of the war the most striking successes came to the South, so for over two years the pro-South sympathisers in this country were able to force their ideas to the front, and to give a wholly unjustifiable appearance of strength to their party in England. The period of hesitation between the election of Lincoln and the attack on Fort Sumter, when the North was distracted between its love of peace and its doubts about the right of coercion, and its hatred of secession, had its parallel in this country in the long period of doubt as to whether a Northern triumph would really involve the destruction of slavery. In each case we have what really proved to be by far the strongest factor in the nation, the opinion of the common people, slow to realise the full meaning of the quarrel, slow to attain the unity necessary to secure victory for its idea, slow even to find a definite and coherent expression for that idea itself.

We may take the parallel a little further. Previous to the election of Abraham Lincoln it may be said that both Governments were in the hands of the privileged classes and their friends. Here the Government, whether Whig or Tory, was never representative of the democracy, who only began to influence Parliament directly after 1868; in America, previous to Lincoln's victory, politics were almost wholly controlled by the slave-owning South. Hence, the side of American or British politics presented most clearly to the view of average men in the other was not that of the common people, but of a class. We should not forget that up to Lincoln's administration the actual rulers of the United States were generally convinced friends of slavery, while those of England were anti-republican aristocrats. The latter had a genuine hatred of slavery combined with a strong dislike to seeing a great Republican success. It would have been hard to win their cordial sympathy for the North in any case, for nothing but the success of the South could, in the long run, prevent the Union becoming some day or other the richest and most numerous nation in the civilised world. Even a perfectly clear issue between slavery and emancipation would only have divided their sympathies, and unfortunately it was long before such a clear issue emerged from the conflict.

It would not be fair to assume that the hatred of slavery among the English aristocracy was hypocritical. The British aristocracy in the mass have always been foes to equality, but unlike most other aristocracies they have an honourable record in defence of liberty. Though Magna Carta was enforced by the barons, it asserts firmly enough the rights of the common people, and even as far back as the days of Anselm slavery was prohibited in England. It was due to Anselm that in 1102 the Church Synod at Westminster condemned the " wicked trade used hitherto in England by which men are sold like brute animals." This, of course, does not apply to serfdom, but to chattel slavery, but 1102 is a startlingly early date at which to find any form of slavery condemned.

In a series of articles contributed to *Fraser's Magazine*, the late Mr. F. W. Newman stated that both the African slave trade and slavery itself were "from the beginning utterly illegal, and only gained a show of legality through the malversations and neglects of executive officers, whose real duty it was to suppress it wherever it lay in their power." The patent of Hawkins, the first Englishman to engage in the slave trade, only permitted him to carry Africans to America with their free consent, though he paid no heed whatever to this limitation. The slave trade was never legalised, and the Act in the reign of George II to regulate the trade of Africa contained a strict provision against taking on board or carrying away any African "by force or fraud." Slave-hunting ship captains, however, were well out of reach of the officers of the law, who on their part made no serious effort to interfere with them, and the monstrous system grew up under the British flag without the sanction of British law and in defiance of the Constitution.

As the common law of England applied to the American colonies, it seems doubtful whether slavery was ever strictly legal even in the United States! Mr. Mason of Virginia, when the Fugitive Slave law was pending, objected to fugitives being brought before a jury, because it would bring up the legality of negro slavery, which, he said, "it would be impossible to prove." Congress, therefore, struck out the jury trial!

How the law stood on the subject was first fully tested in the case of the negro Somerset. Here is Newman's account of the matter :—

"A planter brought to London a slave called James Somerset, in 1772, and when he fell ill, inhumanly turned him out of doors. Mr. Granville Sharp, a philanthropic barrister, found him in the street, placed him in a hospital where he recovered his health, and then got him a situation as a servant. Two years after, his old master arrested and imprisoned him as a runaway slave. Mr. Sharp brought the case before the Lord Mayor, who ordered Somerset to be set at liberty. But the master seized him violently in the presence of the Lord Mayor and Mr. Sharp; on which the latter brought an action against the master for assault. The question of law was finally referred to the twelve judges, in February and May of that year, who decided *unanimously*, that no man can be accounted a slave on English territory. This decision is often quoted, as though the *soil* of Great Britain made a slave free; but that is a legal fiction. Evidently, it is only when a slave (so called) comes *within the reach of an English court* that his freedom is declared. At that time the American colonies were beginning their quarrel with Great Britain, but had not renounced allegiance. All the colonies were subject to the common law of England, and if in Virginia and Jamaica there had been a judge as upright and able as Lord Mansfield and a philanthropist as zealous as Granville Sharp, it would seem that slavery might have been dissolved by a few judicial trials."

Whatever their other faults, the English aristocracy have ever been as strong defenders of certain fundamental principles of liberty as any other class, and even to-day there is no Member of Parliament who can be more certainly relied upon to resist, not only with earnestness but with passionate eloquence, any encroachment on what he considers the basis of liberty than the Tory aristocrat, Lord Hugh Cecil.

To a large extent, no doubt, the planters of the West Indies and of the Southern States carried on the tradition of their fathers in the old country. Even the slave-owners themselves for long looked forward to ultimate emancipation, which they regarded as necessary and right, however difficult. The moral apologetic for slavery came later, and only after the planters had been corrupted by generations of slave-owning and by the profits of cotton growing. The same degradation was, no doubt, common to our West Indian slave-owners and those of the United States, and the reason why the system was got rid of with comparative ease in the British Empire, while it was only ended after such a tremendous conflict in the Republic, is that the slave-owners had very little political influence on the British Parliament, while they controlled the Government and were deeply entrenched in the Constitution and the social order of the States.

The clear conviction, then, that slavery was the real point at issue, or that the conflict involved the continuance or destruction of the system, would have gone far to enlist for the North the sympathy even of the classes who became, as a matter of fact, their bitterest opponents. I fear, however, that, slavery apart, these classes were on every other issue involved certain from the first to favour the South. The " call of the blood " was, for them, much stronger from the South, just as that from the North was more potent for the masses. The new belief in free trade, and the old narrow jealousy of the prosperity of rival nations, tended to bring sympathy to States whose bias was towards freedom of exchange, and to any project which would weaken the young Republic. America was then our greatest rival in shipping, and seemed likely enough ere long to deprive us of our leadership on the seas. It seemed, too, that with a divided America Canada would be more secure; and though this view of the case overlooks the fact that a divided America would certainly be an armed America, whereas the united Republic maintained only a nominal army, I think there is little doubt that it was widely held. Above all, there was a dislike to republican institutions, natural to people who had or hoped to have titles, and a pretty general wish to see the " Republican bubble burst." On his meaner and narrower side the Tory or Whig aristocrat could easily be appealed to by the South; the claims of the North to that which was nobler in him was nothing like so clear until long after he had definitely given his sympathies to the other side.   But for the slavery question, of course, there would have been no Civil War, and this being so it is difficult for us to realise how people could believe that the war had nothing to do with slavery. Yet nothing is more certain than that many people in England who were genuine opponents of slavery, men with such honourable records on the subject as Brougham and Russell, quite failed to see that the South was fighting for slavery and at bottom for nothing else. Nor was their blindness so inexcusable as it appears to us. In the manifestos of the Southerners themselves, indeed, the thing is clearly enough stated.   Their " peculiar institution " was no longer safe with an anti-slavery President in power, but Southern agents in England were astute enough to keep this in the background, while the leaders of the North itself were doing all they could to convince the world that slavery was not in danger. They were, indeed, in a difficult position. The Federal Government had no constitutional power, however strong its will might be, to abolish

slavery; had Lincoln proposed to do anything of the sort, it would have been he and
not the South who was breaking the Constitution. Until the South aroused the passion
of the North by firing on the United States
flag, the prevailing feeling among the people
of the free States was all in favour of peace
at any price that could preserve the Union.
Many, indeed, were not confident that, however hateful such a policy might be, a State
was not within its legal right in seceding.
The Constitution is not very definite on the
point, and as a mere legal matter perhaps as
much can be said for one side as for the other
in the quarrel. Many, even those who were
confident that secession was unconstitutional,
were not at all clear as to the Federal Government's right to coerce a rebellious State.[1]
Certainly no provision is made in the Constitution itself for the coercion of any State
wishing to secede, and Americans having a

---

[1] It will, I think, often be found in civil or other wars
that the side most in the wrong in essentials has at least
as good a case from the purely legal point of view as its
opponents. The wish for peace and conciliation is all
to the credit of the North, but this legal scrupulosity
seems hardly justifiable. The Constitution hardly
needed to make special provision for such a case, as
any Government must be presumed to have the right to
defend its existence.

most amazing reverence for law and the Constitution, Lincoln had a very difficult task before him to evoke the enthusiasm of his side until the South proceeded from mere peaceful secession and fired on the United States garrison. From that point, of course, the North had as good a case for war as it would have had against any foreign Power who did a similar thing, and the attack on Fort Sumter drew the North together as one man, and brushed away all the constitutional scruples that up to then impeded action.

And in truth the North was not prepared to overthrow slavery. It had already made many compromises to avoid the disruption of the Union, and it certainly would not have supported Lincoln in any definite attack on the established rights of the slave States themselves. What Lincoln was pledged to do was to resist the *extension* of slavery into the territories controlled by the ` Federal Government itself, so that no more slave States should be formed; to limit the area of slavery, not to abolish it.

The President's position obliged him, therefore, to disclaim as emphatically as possible any intention to interfere with slavery, and by doing this he undoubtedly strengthened his position in the United States. But perhaps it was inevitable that these disclaimers should have a very bad effect on British opinion. We can see now how disastrous it would have been to the world, as well as to the United States, if the Union had been broken; but the full extent of the disaster has perhaps only become apparent to us in the great war just ended. Because she remained united, America has been able to interfere decisively in the European conflict; while for the same reason she is now in a position to preserve the Old World from anarchy. At the time of the Civil War such a consequence of the victory for the North could have been foreseen by nobody, and the political question of union or secession must have appeared almost purely an American one. Only by bringing in the slavery issue, and thus transforming a question of American politics into a great moral issue was it possible to arouse the moral forces of Europe, and to generate a strong enthusiasm for the cause of the North.

If this be a correct interpretation of the position, British sympathy during the Civil War took a course which, however deplorable, might have been expected. At the outset only a very small number of people understood the question at all. How many in this country even to-day could give any clear account of American domestic politics or, for the matter of that, of those of any other country but their own? It is never reasonable to expect a clear understanding of a foreign question until opportunity has been given for much discussion of the matter from both sides. The moral issue of slavery or abolition was, of course, the same both in the United States and in the British dependencies, but the circumstances in the two cases were so different and in one so complex, that only by a long preliminary instruction in American affairs was it possible to the average Englishman to see why the North should not immediately proclaim the emancipation of the blacks, or how, if such a declaration were not forthcoming, the slaves would be any worse off in a victory of the South.

A few only—whose close study of American politics or whose correspondence with American Abolitionists had taught them what those who had carried Lincoln to victory at the polls, and the South who had bitterly opposed him alike fully understood, that

Southern slavery if it were to continue at all must expand—saw clearly that victory for the North must ultimately mean the destruction of the system. The Civil War came as the climax to the long struggle between those who were fighting for the extension of slavery as a necessary condition of its permanence even where it was already established, and those who were trying to confine it within its original bounds. Lincoln, as the South said, would not hew down the tree of slavery, he would only bind it round with a circle of iron so as to strangle its life. Probably they were right, and at least in this most enemies of slavery in the Northern States agreed with them; for though at the stage of growth to which the Union had then developed it was impossible to get the two-thirds majority in the Senate and Congress necessary to pass an amendment to the Constitution abolishing slavery, the Northern States were increasing so much faster in population than the South that a great free soil majority in the Congress was certain sooner or later. When that came about the only protection for the slave-owner would be the Senate, the majority in which would depend, not on the whole population, but on the relative number of slave and free States. It seemed, therefore, vital to the slave-owners that the number of slave States should increase as rapidly as those where slavery was prohibited, and that the undivided territories directly under the control of the Union out of which new States would be carved should be open to slavery. The motto of Lincoln that slavery was sectional, not national, and should not be permitted in territory directly under the control of the Federal Government was only a method of preparing the way for the ultimate constitutional abolition of slavery. The only way to prevent abolition was to secede from the Union, and this and this alone was the cause of secession.

But while keen students of American affairs like Cobden, professors of history like Goldwin Smith, and active propagandists of abolition like George Thompson, might understand this, the general public here could not be expected to know anything about it. For their guidance at first there was only the palpable fact that an army of free men was fighting against an army of slave-owners. That seems to have been enough for the British working classes who never from the first supported the South. But the leading organs of public opinion were almost all on the other side, contending that after all the controversy was not about slavery. This the people were in no position to dispute, especially as so far as they could see the Northern leaders seemed to admit it. Before a stubborn refusal to join in the pro-South demonstrations of statesmen and journalists could give place to a fervent support of the North, it was necessary for such men as created the Union and Emancipation Society to explain the real position to them, or for Lincoln himself to develop the policy of abolition, which as the war progressed became possible to him. When at last it became clear that the triumph of the North would mean the end of slavery, there was, as we shall see, no lack of enthusiasm among the working people of this country. Then they realised that the cause of the North was the cause of freedom the world over, and if not in the Press in their public meetings made their voices clear.

Meantime, however, serious harm had been done, not only to the cause of the North, but to the friendship of the English-speaking peoples. We can recognise that when the

North confidently anticipated the enthusiastic support of an anti-slavery country of the same blood and speech as itself there was an element of unreason in the anticipation. If the masses here did not see their difficulties, neither did those of the North understand how the whole issue was not clear to us. They could hardly be expected to remember, excited as they were by the strain of the war, that even they themselves had been slow to recognise the true character of the struggle. Nor did they know that just as the South had gained the advantage of the first blow in the opening stages of the struggle and had captured the arsenals of the United States itself, so the pro-South minority in this country held the great newspapers and all the means of public expression in their hands. The voice of *The Times* was no more that of England than that of the South was that of America, but just as from the early successes of the Secession many people here expected the ultimate victory of the Slave Power, so from the cackle of the pressmen and the clubs America judged the feeling of England. However disastrous, it could hardly be otherwise. Nations must judge one another by appearances, and it was long before there was any apparent sympathy in this country for the cause of the North.

But nothing is more exasperating than to be refused sympathy in trouble from any quarter to which you have confidently looked for it. Whenever a great war occurs, difficulties are sure to arise between belligerents and neutrals. War is an anti-social state of things; it is in its essence the negation of law. As soon as war is proclaimed, the belligerent immediately proceeds to do many things which it would be an unpardonable crime against international law for any one to do in peace. "Belligerent rights," as concerns neutrals, are one and all merely "rights" to break the law of nations, and the codes drawn up to define them are illogical compromises between any decent rule of international law and belligerent necessities. I take it there never has been and never will be real agreement between belligerent and neutral as to the rights of war : the belligerent will always be struggling to extend, and the neutral for the time being to limit them. Even when some crude compromise has been agreed to, or some tolerable rule laid down in the text-books, ignorant or headstrong officers will do rash or defiant things, which will need careful and considerate handling by statesmen. In the American Civil War, as in others, many things occurred to produce friction between the English-speaking nations, and twice the countries seemed dangerously near to war. It was not these incidents, however, that mattered; it was not they that embittered to so great an extent the feelings of the American people towards ourselves. The only important practical injury received by either nation from the other was the release of the *Alabama*, with the consequent widespread damage to American shipping. But the incidents which created serious friction in the war, did so mainly because there was a bitter state of feeling already. Had it been possible for Great Britain to express forcibly the deep underlying sympathy of her common people for the great human and national interests which were involved in the cause of the North, the incidental difficulties arising out of the blockade, or any other measure of the war, would not have availed to check the rapid growth of affection and sympathy between the English-speaking nations, a sympathy unhappily deferred for over fifty years.

CHAPTER II

FEELING IN 1861

THE important dates to keep in mind in the year 1861 are April 13th, that of the attack on Fort Sumter; July 21st, that of the battle of Bull Run; and November 8th, the date of the *Trent* affair. Up till the attack on Fort Sumter, there existed throughout the loyal States of the Union a curious hesitation and uncertainty. With growing alarm the North watched State after State seceding from the Union, without forming any very definite idea of the course that ought to be taken. The idea of separation was hateful to them, but so, too, was that of civil war. Buchanan, the retiring President, thought secession illegal, but apparently considered that any attempt to resist secession by force was illegal also. The letters sent to *The Times* by Mr. Russell in these early months present a curious picture of uncertainty in the public mind, and though

Russell's personal sympathies were with the North, he seems to have felt something of contempt for a nation that did not appear prepared to fight for its own existence. This was very bad for the cause of the North in England. It is hard to feel strongly for a people who do not appear to feel strongly themselves, and when once Mr. Russell had revealed to British readers how uncertain the Americans themselves were as to their rights under the Constitution, it was very difficult for our people to understand the vehement patriotism and enthusiastic conviction in the righteousness of the Union cause which followed so quickly the indecision of March and April. Mr. Charles Francis Adams, in the biography of his father, American Minister in London during the war, has given a graphic description of the confusion and uncertainty of the period from November 6th, 1860, when Lincoln was elected, to March 4th, 1861, when he was installed in the White House. " A community," he says of the North, " fairly agonised with fear was being slowly educated to the fighting pitch. The retiring President, Buchanan, gave no lead, but calmly watched while the arsenals of the United States were taken over by the Secessionists in order that they might be ready for use against the Federal Government itself."

In another work Mr. Adams has given us a graphic picture of the uncertainty of the time when, in the winter of 1860 and 1861, State after State was passing ordinances of secession. The danger was that Virginia, and with it the Border States, would secede before Lincoln was inaugurated in March. " Maryland," he says, " would invariably follow the Virginian lead; the recently elected President had not yet been inaugurated; *taken wholly by surprise, the North was divided in sentiment ; the loyal spirit of the country was not yet aroused.*" The italics are mine; and the sentences show clearly what kind of report English visitors might be expected to send home of the state of feeling in America, and how strangely the vehement patriotism and demand for sympathy of a few months later must have seemed to us. If Mr. Justin Macarthy correctly recalls the time, British sympathy at first was heartily with the North. He tells us that " at first the feeling of Englishmen was almost unanimously in favour of the North. It was thought that the Southern States would be allowed quietly to secede, and most Englishmen did not take a great interest in the matter, or, when they did, were inclined to regard the Southerners as a turbulent and troublesome set, who had better be permitted to go off with their peculiar institution and keep it all to themselves."

But, of course, as was amply proved later, the hesitation of the North was due to a feeling inevitable even to the most resolute and bravest people on the brink of a catastrophe as terrible as unexpected. There was no real indifference, only a nerve-shaking suspense, which would be transmuted later on to a passionate self-assertion, difficult and even dangerous to deal with. Americans saw before them the danger of a national humiliation, the depth of which it is perhaps necessary to be an American to understand. In no country in the Old World are senti-ments of national pride and patriotism so intimately bound up with the political con-stitution of the nation as in the United States. In Europe such feelings gather round the traditions, literary, artistic and historic, of the past; in America, to a far greater extent, they are bound up with the future. The American Constitution is felt to be, not a heritage of the past, but a model for the

future; a thing to which it will be the pride
of Americans to see the Old World gradually
conform. Its combination of freedom with
strength, of local independence with national
unity, is a just object of pride to the citizen
of the United States. That during three
generations it had stood secure was a guarantee
to him that his fathers had really given a
model to the world; it was a great contribution to civilisation, the standing justification
of his nation. If it failed, if it were broken by
disruption, everything failed. The American
had no long record of success behind him, to
which he could appeal for the verdict of
posterity. Removed from the conflicts of the
Old World, he instinctively saw that it was
not by taking part in the competitive politics
of Europe, but by giving to Europe and the
world a new political idea and by making it
a success on a grand scale, that he could
secure that world recognition to which he
felt the greatness of his nation entitled him.
The people of the United States were engaged
in a world task of the utmost importance,
the subduing to civilisation of half a continent, perhaps the richest and best three
million square miles of land in the globe.
Great as this task was, however, it was not

in itself enough to win for any nation a prominent place among those who have led the world in philosophy, science, religion, art or literature. To set the pace in solving the problem of federal democracy and universal toleration was to make such a contribution, and the soul of America longed to justify itself by making it.

In the work of the greatest and most American of her poets that claim was even then being made with uncouth power well suited to this theme, if to no other. We enter into the spirit of America at the time of the Civil War in the poetry of Walt Whitman. In the poet of democracy we see revealed the passion that lay hidden beneath the doubt and hesitation of which Mr. Adams speaks. Its defects are the defects of America at the time, but its ideals are the ideals of America also; it is the new poetry of the New World.

It was, of course, impossible for the British people to feel towards the crisis as the Americans did. They were at first aware only of the strange apparent apathy already noted; they were quite unprepared for the outbreak of passion which followed on the attack and surrender of Fort Sumter. We

can gather the effect that this incident had
upon the North by the similar effect produced
here by the German invasion of Belgium.
Substitute for the suspense of the twelve
days of vain struggles for peace a similar
suspense of as many weeks while State
followed State in secession, while the change
took place from a doubtful, almost treacherous
administration to one loyal but untried and
almost unknown, and we can realise how one
striking event, a shot fired in anger on the
flag, could crystallise the gathering wrath of
America and make it solid and resolved.
But it is not strange that our ancestors did
not understand this.   In a moment America
forgot even her immediate past; no longer
hesitating, she forgot her recent hesitation,
and clamorously called for the sympathy of
the world.

South Carolina seceded from the Union on
December 20th, 1860, being the first State to
do so.   On December 26th, Major Anderson,
commander of the United States forces in
Charleston Harbour, moved his small garrison
from Fort Moultrie to Fort Sumter on an
island in the harbour.   Here, unless he was
relieved, his garrison would sooner or later
starve, and an attempt was made in the

following month to relieve him with supplies and reinforcements. The people of Charleston, however, fired upon the ships and prevented the relief being effected. The situation remained unchanged till April 13th, six weeks after the inauguration of Lincoln, when the Secessionists opened fire on the fort. The South had begun the war by firing on the American flag. " From that moment," says Mr. Adams, " the loyal North was a unit."

There succeeded a period of delirious confidence. It almost seems as though, in accepting the gage of battle, the North had resolved to lose sight altogether of the magnitude of its task. Lincoln called for 70,000 volunteers, and these came at once and enthusiastically at his call. Nor was it realised how inadequate such a force would be. We had the miscalculation that seems inevitable at the outset of all great wars; only through failure and tribulation the nations come to realise the full extent of any first-class struggle. From the fall of Fort Sumter, on April 13th, to the battle of Bull Run, in July, we may reckon the second stage of American opinion, that of assured self-confidence, in which the nation, angry at the outrage committed upon it, but antici-

pating an early and easy victory, is somewhat
arrogantly inclined to expect immediate sympathy from foreigners, and not very willing
to conciliate the opinion of those who delay
to give it.

It was here that the first hitch in the
relations of the two countries begins. On
April 19th the North proclaimed the whole
Southern coast in a state of blockade. This
proclamation rendered it imperatively necessary for foreign Governments, especially our
own, to define their attitude towards the war.
This is now admitted by reasonable Americans,
though some of them still complain of the
promptness with which this country and
France accorded " belligerent rights " to the
South. To me even this objection seems
invalid. A state of war had come into existence between South and North, of which the
proclamation of the blockade was an admission. By reason of the blockade the North
claimed and at once exercised " belligerent
rights," which would be admittedly intolerable
in time of peace, to search, stop and confiscate
the shipping of foreign Powers. It is admitted that such a state of things could not
endure for any length of time without some
definite recognition of the rules under which

it was carried on, and no such definition was possible until the state of war was recognised. If British ships had been stopped and searched continually in time of peace, or when a fiction of peace was kept up, the tension which existed all along during the war between the Powers would have been ten times worse, and armed intervention would have been inevitable. There is nothing to be gained by not recognising a fact, and belligerency was a fact which it was desirable to recognise as soon as it occurred. The early recognition of belligerency was, however, a grave cause of offence to the American people, then naturally in a highly irritable and excited condition. Neither man nor nation when engaged in a life or death conflict can be expected to weigh up the pros and cons of every action taken by the looker-on, especially if, as in our case, he is as much inclined to offer criticism as he is to deny help. Accordingly, when Mr. Adams, the newly appointed Minister of the United States for London, arrived in England, he was much perturbed to find that our Government had already recognised the belligerency of the South and had proclaimed our neutrality. He was one of a long line of admirable diplomatists whom the United States had accredited to London, and he had a trying time before him. It was unfortunate, therefore, that at the outset of his mission he should be met by what he seems to have considered an injurious action on our part. Possibly there may have been already some anti-American feeling in the Cabinet, though we have the evidence of Mr. W. E. Foster, a strong friend of the North, that it was the friends of the Union cause in the Cabinet that pressed for the neutrality proclamation. Why they did so is clear enough : without such a proclamation the blockade itself could not be recognised, and it was of the very last importance to the North that the blockade should be preserved. Mr. Adams, and other American statesmen with him, appear to have thought that the proclamation encouraged the South in their rebellion, which but for this action of ours would soon have collapsed. We can understand, therefore, with what uncomfortable feelings he entered upon his mission. Here he had to deal with an aristocratic Whig Government really opposed to slavery, but by no means friendly to democracy and republicanism, and powerfully influenced by the opinion of a clubland with likes and dislikes very similar to their own, but, unlike themselves, uncontrolled in its utterances by any sense of responsibility. The opinion of the people was as yet confused and inaudible, so that though, when enlightened and aroused, it appeared firmly on the side of the North, it was difficult at the time to distinguish the voice of democracy from that of the London Press and the limited circle whose views it expressed.   Mr. Adams' presence was looked upon as an embarrassment in the social circles among which ambassadors move, and was rarely asked for at their entertainments.   Except to those deeply interested in the issues involved, the war was, as it always is to neutrals, an unmitigated nuisance inflicting real and terrible hardships on the British people.   The gains to be obtained from it for this country were apparently *nil*, and those for humanity by no means clear, so long as the North declined to come out clearly on the side of emancipation.   There developed, too, ere long the apparent probability that the South would succeed, and that we should have to define and explain our relations to a new American Power created by the war.   Looking back at the time between the battle of Bull Run, in

July 1861, to those of Gettysburg and Vicksburg two years later, it seems to me that this
must have appeared to Europeans by far the
most probable result of the struggle. Indeed,
it would be a poor compliment to our
American cousins not to recognise what a
tremendous thing they did in subduing the
slave-holders' rebellion, or to maintain that
in the earlier days of the conflict foreigners
could be expected to foresee the ultimate
result. The revolted States contained many
millions of white people determined and able
in war; they were possessed of a large territory difficult to overrun and subdue. To
conquer such a people completely, so as to
be able to compel their re-entry into the
Union they had left, was a task of immense
difficulty, and it is no wonder, especially
after the early successes of the South, if the
world doubted its possibility. But the success of the South, however regrettable, would
have compelled European nations to enter
into regular diplomatic relations with the
new Power, and might have rendered them
liable to face compensation claims for any
action they took during the war capable of
a hostile or unneutral interpretation. These
considerations were certainly always in the

minds of our statesmen, even of those most friendly to the North. As, however, the North was passionately conscious of its determination and confident of its power to crush the rebellion, considerations of this kind would have been resented with peculiar bitterness. Probably no Northerner dare admit, even to himself, much less to a foreigner, the possibility of ultimate defeat, and nothing could offend him more than to find any one else less sanguine.

Mr. Adams, therefore, had to deal with people largely hostile in feeling, and apparently even more hostile than they were. This was at any rate the case with our Foreign Minister, Lord John, afterwards Earl, Russell. Of him Mr. Adams came to say long after, " I hope I may not be exceeding my just limits if I seize this occasion to do a simple act of justice to that eminent statesman. Much as I may see cause to differ with him in his limited construction of his duty, or in the views which appear in these papers to have been taken by him of the policy proper to be pursued by Her Majesty's Government, I am far from drawing any inferences from them to the effect that he is actuated in any way by motives

of ill-will to the United States, or indeed by
unworthy motives of any kind. If I were
permitted to judge from a calm comparison
of the relative weights of his various opinions
with his action in different contingencies, I
should be led rather to infer a balance of
good-will than of hostility to the United
States ! "

In his biography of his father, as well as
in papers read to the Massachusetts Historical
Society, Mr. C. F. Adams, junior, has called
attention [1] to the serious complications arising
from the state of feeling in the North itself,
and from the policy of Mr. Seward, Foreign
Minister of the Republic. In the period
before the *Trent* affair he tells us that,
" morbidly excited and intensely sensitive,
the country was in a thoroughly unreasoning
and altogether unreasonable condition, very
necessary now to emphasise; for it needed
only the occurrence of some accident to lead
to a pronounced explosion of what can only
be described as Anglophobia." It must be
remembered that in these critical months
there was an anti-British feeling in the
States as strong at least as any feeling, even

[1] See the Transactions of the Society for September
and October 1912.

among aristocratic circles, in England against America.

Unfortunately, it now appears that, whether at other times personally hostile to this country or not, Mr. Seward, the American Foreign Secretary, was only too willing to embroil his country with ours. Mr. Seward did not for long realise the depth of disunion sentiment in the South, nor the strength of the rebellion. It seems clear that he imagined that below all the controversy about State rights there was in the hearts, even of the rebels, a strong sentiment of patriotism, an appeal to which against the foreigner could be relied upon to re-unite the nation. He seems deliberately to have preferred a foreign war to the threatened civil one, and planned to provoke a foreign conflict as a means of curing the domestic quarrel! In a paper submitted to President Lincoln, in April 1861, entitled " Some Thoughts for the President's Consideration," he proposed, in order to divert the public mind, to demand from Spain and France explanations, " categorical and at once," of their proceedings in the West Indian Islands and Mexico. He then proposed to seek " explanations from Great Britain and Russia, and send agents into

Canada, Mexico and Central America to rouse a vigorous continental spirit of independence in this continent against European intervention," and if satisfactory explanations were not received from Spain and France, "to convene Congress and declare war against them." As on so many occasions, the good sense of President Lincoln came to the help of his country. He modified the despatch, which would otherwise, in all probability, have involved the United States in a general war, though even in its altered form it caused Mr. Adams sufficient embarrassment.

Mr. Adams did not know of these designs of Mr. Seward. The British Government were, however, not without strong suspicions in the matter. Lord Lyons, the British Ambassador at Washington, wrote at the time to Lord Russell :—

"Upon receiving the intelligence of your Lordship's declaration in Parliament, Mr. Seward drew up a despatch to Mr. Adams to be communicated to your Lordship in terms still stronger than any he had before used. I fear that the President has consented to its being sent, on condition, however, that it is to be left to Mr. Adams's discretion to communicate it or not, as he may think advisable. If sent, it will probably reach London about the same time with this despatch." [1]

He found Mr. Seward in a state of mind very difficult to deal with. From Mr. W. H. Russell's diary Mr. Adams's son has extracted a picture which gives a vivid idea of this. Mr. Russell wrote :—

" Mr. Seward has been fretful, irritable, and acrimonious; and it is not too much to suppose Mr. Sumner has been useful in allaying irritation. A certain despatch was written last June, which amounted to little less than a declaration of war against Great Britain. Most fortunately the President was induced to exercise his power. The despatch was modified, though not without opposition, and was forwarded to the English Minister with its teeth drawn. Lord Lyons, who is one of the suavest and quietest of diplomatists, has found it difficult, I fear, to maintain personal relations with Mr. Seward at times. Two despatches have been prepared for Lord John Russell, which could have had no result but to lead to a breach of the peace, had not some friendly interpositor succeeded in averting the wrath of the Foreign Minister." [2]

We may thus look upon the period of three

[1] *Transactions of Massachusetts Historical Society*, October 1912, p. 41.
[2] *Ibid.* p. 61.

months between the fall of Fort Sumter and
the first battle of Bull Run as one of growing
hostility in feeling between the leading circles
of this country and the ardent spirits of the
North. This state of things, too, was the
more dangerous inasmuch as the American
Foreign Minister, under some strange illusion,
was actually seeking an occasion for war.
Mr. Seward had been looked upon as the
most likely Republican candidate for the
Presidency, Abraham Lincoln being far less
known. It was most fortunate for America
and the world that the Republican Convention of 1860 surprised the nation by choosing
this " outsider," and that during the first
critical three months Lincoln and not Seward
had the final say.

The battle of Bull Run, on July 21st, 1861,
closes the second period in the psychology of
the Northern States. The fall of Sumter had
ended the period of hesitation; the battle of
Bull Run put a period to that of overweening
self-confidence. It was henceforth clear to
Mr. Seward that the Federal Government
would have quite enough to do to subdue
the rebellious States without complicating
matters by foreign quarrels. His general
management of affairs from this time was as

steady and pacific as before it had been provocative and rash. At the outset of every great war there always seems to be a period of absurd confidence, and the expectations of the people at such times make curious reading in the light of subsequent history. We can remember how confident people were in 1899 that the British army would spend its Christmas in Pretoria, and I can remember very well at the outbreak of the late war men who anticipated that the British flag would fly over Berlin by Christmas 1914. It was with similar feelings of confidence that the Northerners pressed for a speedy advance with new and untried levies to Richmond in 1861, and the premature attempt was made that led to the disaster of Bull Run. From that day, as I have said, we may date the third period in the psychology of the American people, and certainly an improvement in American diplomacy. The danger of America forcing intervention was now but slight. War could hardly now break out, except by the fault of this country.

Of that, however, there was still as much danger as ever; for now the inevitable hardships of the war were beginning to tell in England and France. By September five-sixths of the operatives in certain localities in Lancashire were either altogether unemployed or working half time, and thousands of people were every day added to the number receiving parochial relief. The supply of cotton became less and less and the price of it higher and higher each month. The sufferings of Lancashire were terrible, while the cotton shortage was pressing only less severely on France, whose Emperor was wishful that England would make a move and recognise the South. On this, Jefferson Davis and the leaders of Southern opinion had reckoned as one of the best cards in the game. That "cotton was king," and that the lack of the raw materials for their industry would force the Powers of Europe to intervene and break the blockade, was one of the dreams of the Southern President. That it proved to be a dream was due before anything else to the heroism of the cotton operatives. The courage with which they submitted to bear any hardship rather than say anything that would help a rebellion of slave-owners is one of the greatest things in English history, and was no small factor in securing the success of the North. How they met the crisis is well described in Mr. Adams's biography :—

" The extraordinary feature in the situation was, however, the patience of the victims; and the organs of the Confederacy noted with ill-suppressed dismay the absence of ' political demonstrations, to urge upon a neglectful Government its duty towards its suffering subjects, and to enforce at once the rules of international law and the rights of an injured and innocent population.' A distinctly audible whine was perceptible in their utterances. ' It is,' one of them said, ' the great peculiarity of England that the heart of the country is thoroughly religious. The plain issue, then, between the two nations was therefore naturally overlooked by those whose programme in America was the law of conscience overriding the law of the land; and the prominence they gave to the slave question was especially directed to the religious public in England. And well has it answered their purpose. To this very hour the great mass of the people have no other terms to express the nature of the conflict. . . . It is to no purpose that argument, fact, and experience have shown the utter indifference of the North to the welfare of the negro; the complete appreciation by the slaves themselves of the sham friendship offered them; and, still more, the diabolical preaching of the ministers of God's word, who rely on Sharp's rifles to carry out their doctrines. The emancipation of the negro from the slavery of Mrs. Beecher Stowe's heroes is the one idea of the millions of British who know no better, and do not care to know.' In truth, the fundamental sin of the Confederacy had found it out. Literally, and in no way figuratively, the curse of the bondsman was on it. Rarely, indeed, in the history of mankind, has there been a more creditable exhibition of human sympathy, and what is known as altruism, than that now witnessed in Lancashire. The common folk of England, Lincoln's 'plain people,' workless and hungry, felt what the wealthier classes refused to believe, that the cause at issue in America was the right of a working man to his own share in the results of his toil. That cause, they instinctively knew, was somehow their cause, and they would not betray it. So no organised cry went up to break the blockade which, while it shut up cotton, was throttling slavery." [1]

Of this devotion of the cotton operatives the mass of the American people knew nothing, or at least much less than they did of the bitter tone of the London Press and the cold neutrality of the British Government. To them the year from the election of Lincoln to the *Trent* affair, in November 1861, was one long humiliation. They were sore at heart and bitterly resentful, not only

[1] *Charles Francis Adams*, by his son, C. F. Adams, pp. 271, 272.

against the rebels, but with an unsympathetic world. Instead of becoming first among the nations, the pioneers of a world democracy, their nation was in danger of sinking into insignificance. They longed for some striking event, some act of daring, to give back to the nation its old confidence in itself. Such an occasion was sure sooner or later to come to a gallant people engaged in a gigantic war, nor did it long delay.

The American steam sloop *San Jacinto* had for nearly two years been cruising off the west coast of Africa, engaged in suppressing the slave trade. Returning home, she touched at Cienfuegos, where her commander, Captain Wilkes, learnt that two envoys of the Confederate Government, Messrs. Mason and Slidell, duly accredited to London and Paris respectively, were to embark on the British steamer *Trent*, which was due to leave Havana on the 7th of November. Thereupon Captain Wilkes resolved to stop the *Trent* and take from her the two Confederate envoys. He steamed to the Bahama Channel, through which the *Trent* was bound to pass, and waited there for her coming. On the 8th of November the *Trent* was sighted, and as she approached a shot was fired across her

course, and the United States flag was run
up to the masthead of the *San Jacinto*. The
Trent showed the British colours, but did not
stop her course until a shell was exploded
across her bows. Then she stopped, and a
boat's crew sent from the *San Jacinto* boarded
her. Mason and Slidell were thereupon forcibly taken off the *Trent* and put on board
the *San Jacinto*, the former being then
allowed to proceed on her way. She proceeded to St. Thomas, transferred her passengers to another steamer, and arrived in
Southampton on November 27th. Meantime,
the *San Jacinto* had reached Fortress Monroe
on the 15th, so that the news had been published in the United States twelve days before
it was known in England. There ensued
during the next month or six weeks the
stormiest controversy of the war, a controversy that brought the two nations as near
to open hostility as the far more serious
Alabama controversy that happened later.

Looking back at the *Trent* affair at this
distance of time, one is induced to regard it
as the most farcical incident in the history
of Anglo-American relations. Rarely has such
a storm been raised by an event of so little
importance. What actually happened was

the sort of thing to be expected in every naval war, where, as must always be the case, ship captains, with little or no legal knowledge and a natural enthusiasm for the cause of their country, find themselves called upon to act in an emergency. The heart of humanity goes out to the honest sailor, who boldly takes the law into his own hands, and does without thought of possible consequences what at the moment seems to him good for the cause he has at heart. Nor, so long as his action has not been cruel or inconsistent with the unwritten law of the sea that makes of all men comrades in their struggles with its dangers, have the British people ever been harsh judges of friend or foe. They are as willing to make a hero of the captain of the *Emden* as of the Australian who captured him, however much British commerce may have suffered by his depredations. Nor could the countrymen and admirers of Drake and Raleigh plume themselves very much on their respect for legal niceties at sea. The *Trent* affair was exactly one of those incidents which may occur at any time when some scores of zealous, goodhearted, but not legal-minded ship captains are engaged in policing the seas during war; and while it imposed upon our Government the undoubted duty of demanding the restitution of Captain Wilkes's prisoners, it should never have been made an occasion of ill-will between the nations.

For, indeed, admiration for the sailor's courage by no means binds us to an approval of his law. We hand down from generation to generation the precedents of the law courts, so that a very large part of our legal code is neither more nor less than judge-made law. The justification for this is that such precedents are made by men trained for the purpose, and for the most part giving decisions on matters in which their own interest and feelings are not greatly concerned. But if judge-made law has often been criticised, " sailor-made law " would be intolerable. The only method to avoid serious friction between neutrals and belligerents in time of war at sea is to recognise frankly that sailors are likely to bring plenty of " incidents " of an embarrassing nature for arbitration courts to consider, and to bring everything up for revision by a more competent tribunal than that of the quarter-deck. So long as nothing brutal, like the sinking of the *Lusitania*, has occurred, irregularities, however great, should not be made a ground of quarrel.

Whether Great Britain would have treated the exploit of Captain Wilkes in this spirit if it had stood alone can never be known, though by this time the pro-South sympathisers in the country seem to have persuaded themselves that the contest had nothing to do with slavery, and did not attempt to conceal their sympathy with secession. The incident did not stand alone, however. It supplied just the thing that was wanted to rouse the spirit of the American people, so long humiliated and depressed. The interval of several weeks between the time when the *Trent* affair was known in America and that on which its reception in England was reported there saw a most amazing outburst of American chauvinism. Jurists and statesmen, who should have understood international law and felt their responsibility to the nation, vied with journalists and stump orators, who were perhaps more excusable, not only in admiring Captain Wilkes as a plucky seaman, but in endorsing his action as good international law. Worse still, American orators made it fairly clear that the fact that it was a British ship from which the envoys were taken added to the American zest at the capture. People did everything they could to make the thing

as bad as possible, and to make it difficult
for the British Government to regard it as
the indiscretion of a naval officer, and not a
deliberate insult on the part of the American
Government. On November 26th, 1861, a
banquet was given at Boston in honour of
Captain Wilkes, of which Mr. C. F. Adams,
junior, gives the following account :—

" The speakers on this occasion seemed to
vie with each other in establishing a record
from which thereafter it would be impossible
to escape. For instance, John A. Andrew,
then Governor of Massachusetts, a man really
great but of somewhat impulsive disposition,
had been present in the office of the Secretary
of the Navy when the news of the seizure
came in. Literally swept off his feet, he had
sprung upon a chair and been prominent in
the tumult of cheering which followed the
announcement. He now at this banquet
declared that the act of Captain Wilkes had
shown ' not only wise judgment, but was
marked by manly and heroic success.' He
referred to it as ' one of the most illustrious
services that had made the war memorable ';
and then most unnecessarily capped the climax
of indiscretion by declaring to a delighted
audience ' that there might be nothing left
(in the episode) to crown the exultation of
the American heart, Commodore Wilkes fired

his shot across the bows of the ship that bore
the British Lion at its head.'   On the same
occasion George T. Bigelow, then Chief Justice
of Massachusetts, committed himself to an
almost, though not quite, similar extent.
First he voiced the very prevalent feeling
already referred to, saying : ' In common with
all loyal men of the North, I have been sigh-
ing, for the last six months, for some one
who would be willing to say to himself, " I
will take the responsibility "; and who would
not only say this, but when the opportunity
offered would take the responsibility.'   The
Chief Justice of our Supreme Court then went
on to declare that ' Commodore Wilkes acted
more from the noble instincts of his patriotic
heart than from any sentence he read from
a law book '; adding that, under such circumstances, ' a man does not want to ask
counsel, or to consult judges upon his duty;
his heart, his instinct, tells him what he
ought to do.'   Well might the London *Times*,
in commenting on the affair, observe shortly
after :   ' These   are   wild   words   from
lawyers.' " [1]

While America was boiling over with
patriotic enthusiasm, the news both of Captain Wilkes's exploit and of its reception in
the States was being carried across the

[1] *Massachusetts Historical Society Report*, November
1911, pp. 48, 49.

Atlantic to Europe, where it arrived on
November 27th. Very likely, even if the
news of the seizure had come alone, the pro-
South feeling of the clubmen and journalists
of London, by that time highly developed,
would have been enough to raise an unreasonable storm over here. As things were,
it naturally seemed to most people not only
that Captain Wilkes had done an indefensible
thing, but that all America approved of his
deed, and would be prepared to detain the
envoys even at the cost of war. Immediately
an answering tempest arose in England; the
Government prepared for war, and issued
what amounted to an ultimatum to the North
demanding the release of the Southern envoys.
A few weeks of intense strain intervened,
until it was known that the American
Government would, after all, surrender its
captives. This it did on December 26th, and
what was perhaps the most acute crisis in
the war gradually subsided, leaving, however,
behind it a bitterness of feeling altogether
disproportionate to the original grievance.

One of the strange things about the whole
affair is the importance every one seemed to
attach to the two Southern envoys. Their
mission to Europe, as Lord Palmerston truly

said, was not likely in any way to alter the policy either of this country or of France, and they could not in their most hopeful moments have expected to do so much harm to the cause of the North by their diplomacy here as Captain Wilkes had done for them by their capture.   Yet not only the American people, but Messrs. Mason and Slidell themselves, seemed to regard the capture as an important point for the North.   Mr. Slidell, as was afterwards proved, was a master of intrigue, but even he never served his side better than by being captured in November 1861.

CHAPTER III

DURING the year 1862 the supporters of the South in England appeared to have things pretty much their own way. Many things combined to produce this result. In the first place, I think it is true that the North were being called upon to pay in unpopularity for previous faults of American politics which, if common to both sections, were to a far greater extent due to the South than to themselves. It was an unfortunate fact that ever since the War of Independence this country had been the object of nearly all American anti-foreign and chauvinistic feeling. It was hardly possible for the Americans in those days to quarrel with any European Power except Great Britain, Spain, or perhaps France; while the former was the only great Power with which they had ever been at war. Circumstances, then, almost compelled us to play permanently in

American politics the part, which Spain, France, Russia, Germany have in turn filled with us, of national enemy for the time being. Political oratory was early developed in the United States in the struggle for independence, and naturally the earliest subject-matter was the iniquity of the Britishers. Any feeling that existed in England after the acknowledgment of American independence was very soon buried under a mass of newer interests and newer hatreds, so that English visitors to the States must have been not a little astonished that the misdeeds of George III and his ministers were remembered long after they were dead. An Englishman would be more inclined to regard that monarch as

" an old man
With an old soul and both extremely blind,"

than as a fitting successor of Nero or Philip II, to which bad eminence American oratory sought to elevate him. The self-reliance and love of liberty which tempted the American colonies to insist on independence are all the more admirable because they were roused by oppressions trifling as compared with those that have goaded more sluggish natures into rebellion. At this distance of time we can take a pride in the high spirit of our American colonies without awarding Satanic honours to the monarch who lost them for us. Byron's verdict that the king was hardly worth damnation seems to us the truer judgment on George III. But political oratory and nationalistic journalism are not guided by a nice sense of proportion; and there can be no doubt that American politicians were for generations very greatly influenced by a strong feeling of our wickedness and that of our Government. The national epic was based on the conflict with England, and, as far as the policy of the Republic was not controlled by Washington's advice to keep out of the quarrels of the Old World, it was distinctly anti-British.

For the general anti-British tendencies, sometimes of American deeds and generally of American talk, I think the South much more to blame than the North. In New England the war of 1812 was so unpopular that the people of Boston seem even to have talked of secession, while generally the feeling of the North was far more pacific than that of the South. The aggressive policy in Texas that led to the Mexican war was equally opposed to the feeling of the North, as readers of the *Biglow Papers* know, while the filibustering expeditions in Cuba and Central America, and the Ostend Manifesto [1] were detested by the free States. It cannot be denied, however, that the diplomacy of the young Republic under the Southern ascendancy was often neither courteous nor friendly. The desire of the slave States to extend the area of their " peculiar institution " into Latin America and the West Indies gave Spain and Mexico more reason to complain of injury than we had, but British negro sailors visiting Southern ports were seized and enslaved. Generally, Americans had come to be considered by our ruling classes as a boastful and rather truculent

[1] This was a paper drawn up by three American Ambassadors, Mr. Soulé the Minister at Madrid, Mr. Buchanan (afterwards President) at London, and Mr. Mason at Paris. It practically demanded that Spain should sell Cuba to the States, and not obscurely threatened as an alternative to declare war and to take the island by force. The three " diplomatists," certainly not without the knowledge of General Pierce, then President of the United States, and his Cabinet, met at Ostend and drew up this manifesto. Thus, the official representative of the States in Spain insulted the Government to which he was accredited, those in England and France improperly interfered in the affairs of another Power than those to which they were sent, and all three conspired to place the neutral Belgian Government in a very uncomfortable position.

people, who talked much of liberty while perpetuating slavery. The general impression of American character derived from such experiences created a bad atmosphere for the reception of any evidences of anti-British resentment on the part of the North. The feeling towards America in London clubs was, perhaps, not unlike that of a gentleman of the old school towards a modern youth whom he considers badly brought up and whom he would like to " put in his place." It is a very difficult thing to do when the young man, whose manners it is desired to improve, is prosperous and confident, while blandly unconscious of any necessity for improvement, and so when circumstances combine to render such a process possible, it is hardly in human nature for established dignity to withstand it. The Civil War seemed to give such an opportunity, and I fear aristocratic Britain was from the first only too willing to avail itself of it.

But the most dangerous cause of friction arose from the blockade of the Southern ports. It was the pressure on Europe caused by this that seemed to Cobden the most likely cause of intervention. In the letters recently published in full in Mr. Hobson's book, *Richard Cobden, the International Man*, and written to Mr. Charles Sumner, the chairman of the Senate Committee on Foreign Affairs, Cobden again and again returns to this subject. Writing during the stress of the *Trent* affair, on December 12th, 1861, he says :—

" Is there not another side to this blockade ? Does it not, in a certain sense, aid the other party ? So long as all foreign trade is cut off it gives an excuse to those who are in debt not to pay (and who in the South is not in debt ?). Nobody can press for payment even from those who are able to pay, so long as the blockade furnishes a patriotic excuse for suspending all payments. Everybody, therefore, is relieved from pressure. Meantime the blockade increases the bitterness against the North. But, above all, does it not encourage the South to hope for foreign interference ? Then, the negroes being withdrawn from the cultivation of cotton makes labour more available for defensive works. And the whites, having no profitable occupation, turn out to fight. These are points worth your consideration.

" There appear to me only two ways in which you can expect to subdue the South : either by great military operations in the field, or by a sort of armed truce by which you refuse to acknowledge the South, but take your own time to wear out your adversary, leaving it to slavery to do its work for you. But either of these courses must take a long time. As for your expeditions along the coast, you must withdraw the Northern troops next summer, or they will share the fate of our Walcheren Expedition. The South know this, and of course reckon on it. The great Napoleon, in his correspondence with his brother Joseph, seems to treat with contempt these coasting expeditions. If you are to rely on great operations in the field, it is, of course, desirable that you should not be hurried forward from the necessity of doing something to meet the impatience of foreign Powers. You are thus liable to be tempted to precipitate measures.

"By raising the blockade, except for articles contraband of war, you get rid of all pressure from abroad, and the tone of public feeling in Europe would naturally become favourable to the North. *It is the suffering and misery that your blockade is bringing on the masses in Europe that turns men against you.* How can you hope to have a blessing on your cause from those on whom you are inflicting such misery? "

Our Government did not wish, he thinks, nor would our people tolerate any interference on account of such incidents, if the misery and loss occasioned by the blockade did not exist as a genuine grievance. We would have been content with less than the unconditional surrender of the prisoners which we afterwards obtained, and he gives a striking picture of the favour with which arbitration was being considered. Writing on January 23rd, 1862, he says :—

" But it is right you should know that there was a great reaction going on through this country against the diabolical tone of *The Times* and *Post* (I suspect stockjobbing in these quarters). The cry of arbitration had been raised and responded to, and I was glad to see the religious people once more in the field in favour of peace. Be assured, if you had offered to refer the question to arbitration, there could not have been a meeting called in England that would not have endorsed it. The only question was whether we ought to be the first to offer arbitration. I mean this was the only doubt in the popular mind. As regards our Government, they were, of course, feeling the tendency of public opinion. . . . A friend of mine in London, a little behind the scenes, wrote to me, ' They are busy at the Foreign Office hunting up precedents for arbitration very much against their will.' I write all this because I wish you to know that we are not so bad as appeared at first on the surface."

But the *Trent* affair had left a bad feeling behind it, and during 1862 both those who welcomed and those who abhorred such a result were generally becoming convinced that the South would succeed in establishing its independence. Looking back at the time it seems to me that this was almost inevitably the conclusion to which people not gifted with prophetic insight, and not inspired with the national enthusiasm of the Americans themselves, were bound to come. Ten million people, of heroic courage and determination holding a territory of many hundred thousand square miles, were fighting a defensive battle on interior lines against a power larger and stronger, it is true, but to all appearance less martial, and so far apparently less successful. It might well seem that, whether we liked it or not, we should soon have to treat with a new republic well armed and victorious which would call us to account for any friendliness to the North shown in the day of its trial.

It is true, that Lincoln, the sagacious, was steadily feeling his way towards emancipation; but the millions of British people to whom a proclamation of freedom would have swept away every other consideration knew nothing of that. All that they could see was that he made no sign, while thousands of Lancashire families were starving for want of the cotton which the Northern blockade prevented from coming. Even the few who really understood the difficulties in his way, and how necessary it was for him to convince his countrymen that union and emancipation were parts of the same cause before he could decree the end of slavery, must have felt that everything was going against them. How clearly Englishmen who had studied America at first hand could understand the position is shown in a book, *Slavery Doomed*, published in 1860 and written by F. M. Edge and dedicated to Lord Brougham. When the last chapter of this book was written the Republican party had already chosen Mr. Lincoln as their candidate for the presidential election. The author, after predicting with confidence Lincoln's election, says :—

" The Southern States forebode the result and are avowedly preparing to resist. Will their resistance take the form of sullen discontent, or of open opposition to the Federal Government and to the Northern States, so much their superiors in wealth, population, and intelligence?

" The policy of the Slave States with regard to the general Government, is represented by three parties : Unionists, Disunionists, and Nullifiers. The day has gone by for nullification. In the days of Calhoun, its apostle, it was treason to the Constitution ; but nullification has become *too conservative* for the South, and the pro-Slavery leaders are, almost to a man, declaring for secession. Is there sufficient patriotism and common sense amongst the inhabitants of that section, who do not make politics a trade, to prevent the disunionist cabal carrying their plot into effect ? We trust so, but ' the wish is father to the thought.' The Legislatures of the Slave States are more or less disunionists, and the Executives belong to the same category. Legislatures and Executives are elected by the people, and we can only infer that the people who elected them advocate the same principles."

The book then predicts the victory of the North, " to question the result would be to doubt in God and civilisation," it says, and concludes with a prophecy that the result would be emancipation. The political prophet is not often so near the mark ; but it is very seldom that he studies the conditions of a problem so closely as this writer had done.

This quotation is taken from a copy of

his book presented by the author to Mr. Cobden some three years after its publication, at a time when Lincoln's emancipation policy was fully developed and the enthusiasm of the British democracy had been thoroughly aroused on the side of the North. In that year, too, the tide of battle had turned in favour of the Union cause, and a victory for the South was rapidly becoming less and less likely. One wonders how the author felt during the dark days which we are at present considering. Did he, too, ever begin to doubt, when Lincoln had not shown his hand and the clamant minority of clubmen and politicians controlled the British' Press?

There was enough to try his faith. The year 1862 saw little improvement in the progress of the Northern armies, and, indeed, ended in the disastrous battle of Frederickburg. But there was a more serious matter from the point of view of Anglo-American relations even than the ill success of the North, or the delays, necessary under the circumstances, of Lincoln. In July 1862 the most famous of the Southern cruisers, the *Alabama*, was launched at Liverpool, and immediately began to spread destruction among the merchant ships of the North. Unlike the *Trent* affair, this was not a trivial incident, magnified into importance by irresponsible orators on either side of the Atlantic. On the contrary, it was by far the greatest practical injury which this country ever permitted its subjects to do to the American nation. The widespread injury to American shipping which resulted must have had a great deal to do with the relatively insignificant part played by the United States in ocean-going traffic ever since. No doubt, had it not been for the absurd system of high protection followed by the States ever since the Civil War, the large native supplies of iron and other materials in the country and the abounding energies of the people would have very soon assured to them a large share in the shipping of the world, in spite of the change which rapidly followed the war from wooden to iron ships. But the tariff only prevented recovery from a bad position caused largely by the depredations of the Southern cruisers, built in British yards. American shipowners were presented with the alternative of placing their vessels under foreign flags or seeing them sent to the bottom by the *Alabama*.

This was not the sort of grievance that could be adjusted by apology or explanation, and as all the world knows it was only settled by the Geneva Convention and the payment of £3,000,000 damages by this country.

If America had had her hands free at the time, it would almost certainly have led to war. Though it must not be forgotten that the injury done by the *Alabama* was of quite a different character from all the other subjects of dispute between the countries during the war, inasmuch as it was practical and important and not sentimental or trivial; it was, nevertheless, the outcome and expression of British anti-American feeling. A very large part of the people here rejoiced openly in the successes of the *Alabama*, her crew was English, while the passengers on British liners cheered the *Alabama* when they passed her at sea. The manner in which the thing was done, too, was exasperating. It is not, perhaps, very clear why in international law a neutral should be allowed to sell other instruments of war to a belligerent, while to sell a battleship is a breach of neutrality. Our people could sell guns and other weapons to the North and, whenever they could get them through the blockade, to the South also, without any one having a right to object. Such a traffic was strictly legal, both according to our municipal and to international law. The Foreign Enlistment Act, however, had been passed to prevent the " fitting out, equipping, and arming of vessels for warlike purposes " in foreign quarrels. The legal geniuses of the Crown decided that it being lawful to fit out ships, and also to export arms, whilst being against the law to fit out armed ships, all that was necessary to do was to build the ship, launch her without armament, and then send her guns after her to be put on board at the nearest neutral port! It was with such a mischievous legal quibble that the Crown lawyers managed to confuse Lord John Russell and to keep him hesitating and doubtful while the Confederate agents in England and Messrs. Laird, the shipbuilders, were plotting to run a coach and six through the Foreign Enlistment Act.

Captain Bullock, naval agent for the Confederate Government in Europe, came to England in June 1861, and by August in the same year he had succeeded in getting the keel laid for one cruiser and had entered into a contract with Messrs. Laird of Liver-

pool for the more famous *Alabama*. Nobody
in Liverpool seems to have been in any doubt
as to the destination of the ship, and while
she was being built Mr. Adams, the American
Minister in London, continually " bombarded
the Foreign Office with depositions and other
evidence in regard to her." At last, when
the ship was ready for sea, Lord Russell
determined to detain her. A new case containing conclusive evidence was despatched
to Sir John Harding, the Queen's Advocate,
on which our perplexed Foreign Minister
intended to act. The sequel may best be
given in the words of Mr. Adams's son :
" He (Sir John) just then broke down from
nervous tension, and thereafter became hope-
lessly insane. His wife, anxious to conceal
from the world knowledge of her husband's
condition, allowed the package to lie un-
disturbed on his desk for three days—days
which entailed the destruction of the American
merchant marine; and it was on the first of
these days, Saturday, July 26th, 1862, that
Captain Bullock, at Liverpool, ' received information from a private but most reliable
source that it would not be safe to leave the
ship at Liverpool another forty-eight hours.'
On the following Monday, accordingly, the

Alabama, alias the ' 290,' alias the *Enrica,* was taken out of dock, and, under pretence of making an additional trial trip, steamed, dressed in flags, down the Mersey, with a small party of guests on board. It is needless to say she did not return. The party of guests were brought back on a tug, and the *Enrica,* now fully manned, was, on the 31st, off the north coast of Ireland, headed seaward in heavy weather. A grave international issue had been raised, destined to endure and be discussed throughout the next ten years." [1]

That Lord Russell was really anxious to do right in the matter and was genuinely troubled by the legal and other difficulties in the case seems certain, and he was very angry at being tricked by the Southern agents and shipbuilders who had thus compromised British neutrality. He afterwards very frankly admitted himself to blame for the release of the *Alabama,* but it would be unreasonable to expect the Americans to give much consideration to his difficulties. The effect of the whole affair was a grievous wrong to them, which was only made more

---

[1] *Charles Francis Adams,* by his son, C. F. Adams, pp. 314, 315.

annoying by the legal quibbling by which we endeavoured to excuse it.

Looking back on the case from this distance of time, however, we can see that the difficulties of our Government were real enough, at least that we are not the only people who have found it hard to prevent the agents of belligerents and their sympathisers from compromising their neutrality. There was a strong and blatant pro-South party here, while the agents of the Confederacy were actively and unscrupulously endeavouring to use this country as a base for their own purposes. If, in doing so, they should involve us in a war with the United States, so much the better from their point of view —indeed, they must have hoped to accomplish this. This was no new difficulty for a neutral country to face—the United States has twice at least been in the same position, and if at the outbreak of the present war they succeeded, under President Wilson, in defeating the attempts of the Austrian and German embassies and the " hyphenated Americans " to compromise their relations with the Entente, they certainly failed to do so at the outset of the revolutionary wars. In 1793, Genet, the envoy of the French Republic, attempted, and with considerable success, to do the same thing with the United States as the Confederate rebels did with us in 1861-3—to make a base of their ports for a war in which the States were then neutral. He seems to have had a much more violent anti-British feeling among the people to second him. From American ports he was successful in fitting out privateers to attack British commerce, and in setting up Prize Courts there to condemn British ships. " By the privateers," says Goldwin Smith, who cannot surely be accused of unfriendliness to the Americans, " in conjunction with two French frigates, fifty British vessels were captured, some of them in American waters." " In all his outrages," says the same authority, " Genet was wildly applauded by the Republican masses. When his piratical frigate sailed into Philadelphia flaunting the English colours reversed with the French over them, the whole population of what was then the political capital of the Republic turned out to display its sympathy."

Fortunately, Washington was President of the States at the time, and soon found means to curb M. Genet's activity. He was dismissed from the States, and till the British

Orders in Council brought America into the war as a belligerent, her neutrality was henceforth better preserved. The incident is now only worth remembering as showing how difficult it is to preserve strict neutrality with the active agents of a belligerent working upon the sympathies of any considerable part of the population and bent on making mischief.

Throughout the war it seems clear that the public opinion of America, if not its statesmanship, was affected a good deal by a misunderstanding of European politics. It was not the British, but the French Imperial Government that was most anxious to interfere in favour of the South, and to do it bare justice our Foreign Office was throughout a restraining and not a mischievous influence. Cobden, in his correspondence with Sumner, did his best to correct this dangerous impression. He saw that in France similar economic reasons existed for desiring the ending of the blockade, and in a remarkable letter, dated December 3rd, 1861, he says: " From all I hear from France, the trade of that country is dreadfully damaged, and I feel convinced the Emperor would be supported by his people if he were to enter into an alliance with England to abolish the blockade and recognise the South. The French are inconvenienced in many ways by your blockade, and especially in their relations with New Orleans, which are more important to them in *exports* than to us." [1]

Cobden was then fresh from his negotiations with France which led to the famous commercial treaty, and his knowledge of French politics was certainly not surpassed by any man either in this country or America. In the same letter he tells Sumner that the keynote of the French Emperor's policy was friendship with England. " It is," he said, " because I know the inner policy of the French Government that I could not see without mortification and disgust the shallow antics of some of your official representatives in Paris, at that most lamentable public meeting where individuals, accredited by your Government, invited the Emperor to join you against England to avenge Waterloo and St. Helena ! "

Whatever may have been the feeling of the French nation, there can be no doubt the Emperor himself was anxious for the success of the rebellion. It cannot be said,

[1] *Richard Cobden, The International Man*, by J. A. Hobson (London: T. Fisher Unwin, Ltd.).

however divided and vacillating they might be in their policy, that the British Cabinet had any definite object in view which would be injured by a restoration of the Union. It was otherwise with the Emperor Napoleon. In 1861, when Jaurez, the President of Mexico, had suspended the payment of interest on the debt of that country, the Emperor succeeded in persuading Spain and England to join him in a demonstration to obtain security for the money invested by their subjects there. On obtaining this his allies refused to carry their interference any further, but the French grew more extravagant in their demands, and Napoleon proceeded to instal the Archduke Maximilian, brother of the Emperor of Austria, as Emperor of that country. The design certainly was to bring Mexico permanently under French influence, and could only be carried out at a time when the American Government was in no condition to enforce the Monroe doctrine. As soon as the Republic was at peace within its own borders, an army was moved towards Mexico, the position of the French became impossible, and poor Maximilian was left to his tragic fate. The success of the whole venture, a pet scheme of the Emperor's, was

contingent on that of the South, a result
which he had therefore a clear motive to
desire. It is true that French control of
Mexico, a State in which there were no
slaves, would not have been gratifying to
the Southern Republic if ever it had been
established. Through Southern influence
America had already taken Texas from
Mexico and established slavery there, and
the further extension of its " peculiar institution " southwards was generally understood to be an ultimate design of the Secessionists. The power of the South alone to
carry out such a scheme of aggression would
have been very much less than that of the
whole Union; while the general ignorance
of the politicians on either side of the Atlantic
of the aims of those on the other, which is
such a striking feature of the whole period,
probably hid this danger from the statesmen
of France. Be that as it may, Louis Napoleon
had a very strong motive for desiring the
failure of the North.

The sympathies of the French Emperor
come out very clearly in the record of the
doings of the Confederate agents given in the
ponderous volumes of Mr. John Bigelow's
Retrospections of an Active Life. Among

British politicians of the time, Mr. W. S. Lindsay and Mr. J. A. Roebuck made themselves rather absurdly conspicuous by their enthusiasm for the cause of the South, and in April 1862 the former appears to have paid a visit to France to urge on the Emperor to recognise the Confederacy. He had an interview with the latter, an account of which is given in a despatch from Slidell to the Confederate Foreign Minister, Benjamin, and quoted in full by Mr. Bigelow. From this we may quote the most important points :—

" Mr. Lindsay spoke of the Federal blockade as being ineffectual and not in accordance with the 4th article of the Declaration of the Congress of Paris, and mentioned facts in support of his opinion. The Emperor fully concurred in Mr. L.'s opinion, and said he would long since have declared the inefficiency of the blockade and taken steps to put an end to it, but that he could not obtain the concurrence of the English Ministry, and that he had been, and was still, unwilling to act without it. That M. Thouvenel had twice addressed to the British Government, through the Ambassador at London, representations to that effect, but that no definte response had been elicited. The dates of these representations were not mentioned by the Emperor, but M. Rouher had said to

Mr. Lindsay that the first had been made during the past summer, say in June, and the other about four weeks ago." [1]

That the Emperor was eager enough to interfere if he could is clearly to be seen, but he told the officious pro-South Englishman that

" he could not again address the English Ministry through the official channels without some reason to believe that his representations would receive a favourable response. That for that reason he had been desirous to see Mr. Lindsay; that he was prepared to act promptly and decidedly; that he would at once despatch a formidable fleet to the mouth of the Mississippi if England would send an equal force; that they would demand free ingress and egress for their merchantmen with their cargoes and supplies of cotton, which were essential to the world." [2]

Mr. C. F. Adams, in the biography of his father already frequently quoted, seems to have thought that this country was at this time on the verge of acceding to the Emperor's wishes : " All through the summer of 1862,"

---

[1] From *Retrospections of an Active Life*, by John Bigelow, vol. i. p. 484 (London : T. Fisher Unwin, Ltd.)
[2] *Ibid.* p. 485.

he says, " the Ministers of Napoleon III were pressing the British Government towards recognition, and the utterances of English public men of note were becoming day by day more outspoken and significant." Lord Russell, however, seems to have kept his head very well, and informed Mr. Lindsay curtly that he could not receive any advances from the French Government except through the regular channels. As will appear from the above, the Emperor had been snubbed twice when appealing through them, and was not willing to invite a third failure. Mr. Lindsay's mission came to nothing. Unfortunately, however, the pressure of the Emperor and the very real difficulty created by the cotton famine evidently affected our Cabinet very seriously, for on October 7th, Mr. Gladstone, then Chancellor of the Exchequer, made his lamentable speech at Newcastle, in which he informed his audience that the South " have made an army; they are making, it appears, a navy; and they have made what is more than either,—they have made a nation."

This speech, afterwards deeply regretted by Mr. Gladstone, marks the climax of the pro-South movement in this country.   At an

earlier date it might have been the prelude
to intervention; at any later one it would
probably have been impossible. For a far
more important event than any speech took
place that autumn. By slow and cautious
steps Lincoln had been preparing the way
for his emancipation proclamation and in
September it was published to the world.
The British pro-South Press received it with
a howl of contempt and anger, in which,
perhaps, there was not a little instinctive
fear. It was meant to provoke the horrors
of a servile revolt; it was a hypocritical move
to gain credit by manumission in territories
over which the United States had lost control; it was a mere political move to conceal
the desperate condition of the North, and
was never intended to be put into effect.
But these were only the outcries of a faction
sighting their defeat from afar. The abolition proclamation removed all doubt from
the minds of the British democracy and
rendered intervention in favour of the South
impossible.

CHAPTER IV

THE TURN OF THE TIDE

" SHALL I tell you when it was that the reaction in your favour took place? It commenced with the message of your President on the 6th of March, 1862, when he recommended the passage by Congress of a resolution promising indemnity to the planters of the slave States if, in their State legislatures, they would take means to abolish slavery."—*George Thompson, M.P. for the Tower Hamlets, in a speech at New York, May 10th, 1864.*

" I know nothing in my political experience so striking, as a display of spontaneous public action, as that of the vast gathering at Exeter Hall, when, without one attraction in the form of a popular orator, the vast building, its minor rooms and passages, and the streets adjoining, were crowded with an enthusiastic audience. That meeting has had a powerful effect on our newspapers and politicians. It has closed the mouths of those who have been advocating the side of the South. And I now write to assure you that any unfriendly act on the part of our Government—no matter which of our aristocratic parties is in power—towards your cause is not to be apprehended.   If an attempt were made by the Government in any way to commit us to the South, a spirit would be instantly aroused which would drive that Government from power."—*Cobden's letter to Sumner, February 13th, 1863.*

During the year 1862, President Lincoln was taking cautious steps towards a policy of emancipation.   The Southern States, by their attempt at secession and by withdrawing their representatives from Congress, had themselves rendered this possible.   With the North divided on the question and the South unanimously opposed, it was not possible to carry an amendment to the Constitution of the States abolishing slavery by the requisite two-thirds majority.   The withdrawal of the Southern representatives, however, removed the most reliable defenders of the institution, while indignation at their rebellion and the rapid spread of anti-slavery ideas among a people actively engaged in warfare with a slave power was bound to modify the views of those who had so long been prepared to condone slavery rather than

imperil the Union. That policy had disas-
trously failed, and it was becoming clearer
every day that if the States were ever to be
re-united and to remain so, it could only be
on a basis of freedom. Lincoln himself hated
slavery and, if his first duty was to preserve
the Union, there can be little doubt that he
would welcome an opportunity to destroy it.
The Civil War was, however, an evil hardly
less great than slavery itself, and as long as
there was any chance of avoiding or quickly
ending the war without emancipation or
without an actual *extension* of slavery, he
regarded it, and perhaps rightly, as his duty
to those who had elected him not to close
the door to compromise. His progress towards general emancipation, too, was con-
ditioned by the rate of development in the
public opinion of the North. The North
had vehemently denied that slavery was in
danger; the assertion that it was, indeed,
was the only colourable pretext for the
secession movement. The fact of war, however, while it hides from our view the virtues
of our enemy, naturally throws his vices into
strong relief, and even those Americans who
had felt least concern for the negro before the
war were hardly likely to lose so good an

opportunity as that afforded by their
" peculiar institution " to upbraid the South.

The way in which the anti-slavery education of the North progressed under the
stimulus of war may be seen by the conduct
of General Butler. At the beginning of the
war, the General volunteered to use his
Massachusetts troops to put down slave
insurrections, if any should occur, in Maryland. This was, no doubt, meant to assure
the South that the Federal troops would have
a due respect for their property rights, and
to lessen the danger of Maryland, a slave
State, but one which did not join the rebellion,
seceding. Butler, however, had been a
lawyer in time of peace, and he was astute
enough to perceive the use that could be made
of the slave-owners' contention that the
negroes were " property." Negroes were
used to help the Southern army in various
ways behind the fighting lines. Taking
advantage of this, Butler proclaimed slaves
contraband of war, and opened the gates of
Fortress Monroe to fugitive negroes from the
South. Butler's soldiers driven to welcome
fugitive slaves who had escaped from their
enemies very soon came to sympathise with
them. It is thus, in the words of Lloyd

Garrison's son and biographer that " the anti-
slavery education of the soldiers in the field
and the people at home who were ' no
Abolitionists,' while anxious to save the
Union, began." Mr. Garrison " rubbed this
in," not very generously or wisely, one thinks,
in the *Liberator* :—

" There is nothing," he says, " so pro-
motive of clearness of vision and correct
judgment as to be subjected to wrongs and
insults in our own persons. So long as those
traitors confined their outrages and atrocities
to their helpless, friendless slaves, it was all
well enough, and not at all derogatory to
their character as gentlemen, patriots, and
Christians. They might deprive their victims
of every human right, work them under the
lash without wages, buy and sell them ' in
lots to suit purchasers,' and subject them to
every species of brutal violence as passion
or cupidity prompted, and still not forfeit
their claim to be honest, upright, high-
minded men ! Nay, for Abolitionists to brand
them as robbers of God's poor and needy, and
the basest of oppressors, was to deal in abusive
language, and to manifest a most unchristian
spirit ! For were they not exemplary and
beloved Episcopalian, Presbyterian, Baptist,
and Methodist brethren, whose piety was
unquestionable, whose zeal for the Lord was

worthy of all praise, whose revivals of religion were preëminently owned and blessed of Heaven? Were they not the very pinks of Democracy, and the most courtly and chivalrous of gentlemen? But as soon as they began to seize forts, arsenals, custom-houses, and mints belonging to the general Government, to lay their piratical hands upon Northern property, to repudiate their entire Northern indebtedness, and to trample upon the ' stars and stripes '—then, indeed, another view of their character is taken, and they are suddenly transformed from the most estimable Christian brethren and the staunchest Democratic allies into the meanest of scoundrels and the vilest of robbers." [1]

By the spring of 1862, then, three things had happened :—

1. The Senators and Congressmen most directly interested in slavery had deserted Washington—in other words, the strongest garrison of slavery had quitted its post;

2. It had become clear that the Union could only be restored by force, since the South would agree to no compromise on the slavery question;

[1] *The Life and Times of William Lloyd Garrison*, vol. vi. p. 24 (London : T. Fisher Unwin, Ltd.).

3. With the exception of a rapidly dwindling minority, the people of the North had become Abolitionists.

The way was thus cleared for a new departure in politics. One can see clearly that, in the first months of the war, the most immediate necessity for the Federal Government was to preserve the unity of the North. If Mr. Lincoln had done anything to alienate the sympathy of the large mass of people who were " no Abolitionists, while anxious to save the Union," the cause of the North might have been ruined. As he conceived that his first duty was to preserve the Union, the President felt compelled to put even the great moral question of emancipation aside. When, however, the North became more definitely hostile to slavery, it was possible to deal with a peril to the Federal cause only second to that of discord among the loyalists. However excusable, even inevitable, it may have been, the delay in taking up the slavery question had certainly been the cause of nearly all the unpopularity of the North in foreign countries. The reactionary forces in Great Britain and France, the only nations from which intervention was possible, would never, it is safe to say, have dared to propose intervention in favour of the South once the slavery issue was fairly raised. The chances of war are so incalculable, and the resources of the United States so vast, that we cannot be certain what would have been the result even if the European Powers had intervened, but it seems most probable that in that case the secessionists would have succeeded. The state of public feeling in Europe was, therefore, a matter of very grave consideration for American statesmen; it was, indeed, of hardly less importance than the unity and enthusiasm of the Northern people themselves. Yet the policy necessary to maintain unity at home had permitted very dangerous influences to flourish abroad. That the Ulysses of the North managed to steer his craft between the rock and the whirlpool and to achieve, not only the duty to which he was immediately committed, but the desire of his own heart also, was due to a combination of rare sagacity and good luck rarely accorded to any man. With the North firm for abolition, however, the cause of the Union was now bound up with that of anti-slavery, and with due caution Lincoln began to make advances in that direction.

On the 6th of March, 1862, Lincoln sent a message to Congress in these terms : " I recommend the adoption of a joint resolution by your honourable bodies which shall be substantially as follows :—

" *Resolved*, that the United States ought to coöperate with any State which may adopt a gradual abolishment of slavery, giving to such State pecuniary aid to be used by such State in its discretion, to compensate for the inconveniences, public and private, produced by such change of system." This resolution was carried in the House of Representatives by 85 to 35.

In April the President made a further move. Though the question of slavery was one constitutionally left over to the individual States, the district of Columbia, in which Washington is situated, is directly under the control of the Federal Government. It was, therefore, competent for the United States Government to emancipate the negroes of the district, and an Act to accomplish this was accordingly passed and signed by the President. The maxim accepted by Lincoln that slavery was a sectional and not a national policy was thus emphatically confirmed, and the Federal Government, as such, was henceforth free from guilt in the matter.

Lincoln, however, though even his own Cabinet do not appear to have known it, was elaborating a wider policy. The resolution passed in March had not been followed by legislation, so in July Lincoln laid before his astonished Cabinet a proposal for a proclamation paving the way to complete emancipation. Though the proposal was unexpected, it met with general approval in the Cabinet, except as regarded the time when it should be promulgated. July 1862 was a time of depression for the forces of the North, and it was pointed out to the President that to publish such a manifesto at the moment would make it seem like the desperate effort of a beaten party to gain popularity. Mr. Lincoln was therefore advised to reserve his proclamation until some notable success of the Northern arms should provide a fitting opportunity for publishing it. It therefore remained in his desk until the memorable day, September 22nd, 1864.

The proclamation gave notice of the President's intention to recommend an amendment to the Constitution, providing that all States abolishing slavery before 1900 should receive compensation, and that all slaves who, during the Civil War, had enjoyed actual freedom, should not be returned to slavery. It will thus be seen that the proclamation was still very guarded, and fell far short of the immediate emancipation given by the constitutional amendments carried at the close of the war. Nevertheless, its effect was immediately felt, particularly in this country. This is hardly more clearly shown in the extract from Cobden's correspondence quoted at the head of this chapter than in the furious outburst from the pro-Southern Press here, with which it was at once greeted. It seems as if the Press instinctively realised the terrible exposure with which it was threatened. If, after all, the slaves were to be freed, in spite of all the eloquent protests that slavery had nothing to do with the quarrel, and emancipation really took place, the journalists would have to eat their words with a vengeance. This, of course, they were quite capable of doing. The wheel would sooner or later come full circle and the literary supplement of *The Times*, in reviewing Mr. Hobson's recent book, would come round to the point of blaming Cobden for defective enthusiasm for the Northern cause !

But the process was not pleasant to contemplate, and the Press realised that unless it could contrive to prove Mr. Lincoln a hypocrite, its credit with the public might be destroyed. Indeed, as Cobden said, the attitude of the people soon " closed the mouths of those who had been advocating the side of the South." In fact, the anti-slavery proclamation had something like the effect on the democracy of Great Britain that the fall of Fort Sumter had on that of America. It ended the period of doubt, and made the mass of the people look forward definitely to a Northern victory. A great human issue had been raised, and however little the average Englishman might understand or care about the question of Union, he had no doubt at all about this.

The whole thing is an illustration of a very common feature in our public life. Whenever any new and great issue is raised, the regular organs for the expression of public opinion, Parliament, the Press, the political Clubs, etc., very quickly take a side, and express their view very emphatically. They do so, however, without any of the grounds that render them more or less reliable guides as to the trend of public opinion on the questions that have been long discussed among the people. It is thus possible to have for months, or even for years, an apparently unanimous expression of ideas entirely opposed to those that are really current among the masses. Meantime, the general voice of the people is not heard, indeed, for long there may be no leadership and no clearly formed opinion at all. There is merely an instinctive sympathy with the opposite side of the question to that favoured by the authorities, but a sympathy not formulated in any visible way, offering to the rhetoric of the Press and platform rather a sullen refusal to be convinced than the assertion of an opposing view. In this case John Bull could not prove that the cause of the North meant freedom for the slave; he was in no position to argue the matter with the trained advocates of the South; it was easy to out-talk and confuse him. But while he could not answer, he would not be convinced; his simplicity compelled silence, it did not yield consent. And whatever the Press might say, one thing was clear, the South were slave-owners, while the cause of the North was in the hands of Free States; and whatever rhetorical cobwebs might be woven about it, that to the British mechanic was the central fact of the position. However freedom for the negro was to come, then, it would certainly not be by a victory for the South, and from the very outset of the war the working classes gave no countenance to the South.

As long as public opinion remains thus unformulated and vague, it is perfectly possible for the Press to misrepresent it to any extent. Indeed, it may do so in perfect good faith. The journalist quite naturally comes to think that his opinion is the same as public opinion, to use such phrases as " the people wish," " the people are determined," " the great voice of the democracy demands," when really he has nothing to go upon but his own demands, wishes, and determinations. It would be interesting to collect the utterances of *The Times* in the days before it had become a mere Tory organ, and frankly aimed at expressing the real views of the people, and compare its advocacy with the actual opinions expressed by the electors the first time they had an opportunity. Be that as it may, the vocal part of the nation has often gone on voicing one thing with the utmost confidence while all the time as events showed the silent masses have quietly been developing a totally different set of ideas. The awakening when it comes is apt to be startling, and very confusing to the eloquent pressmen whom it exposes.

So it was in the present case. " The people," John Bright said, in a letter to Mr. Bigelow, " have never been wrong. The ' Upper ' class has its newspapers in London always ready to speak out, and they make such a noise that for a time nobody else is heard." He thinks, however, that it was " not so much a change of sentiment as expression of sentiment hitherto concealed " that broke forth throughout the country in the early months of 1863. If, however, the people had " never been wrong," they owed much to the efforts of those few Englishmen who had studied American affairs closely enough to understand the question at issue, and during the dark days of 1861 and '62 had been steadily educating them. It is to be regretted that no full account is now possible of the labours of the Union and Emancipation Society and other pro-North organisations which worked so hard and so successfully to form an enlightened public opinion about the contest. From such of its publications as we have been able to obtain, it is possible to give only a rough idea of the Union's work.   It performed a valuable work for Anglo-American friendship, the knowledge of which may not be without its uses even at this late day.

The founder of the Union and Emancipation Society was Mr. Thomas Bayley Potter, a prominent Lancashire business man and a great friend of Cobden.[1]   In a letter of introduction to the American Ambassador and the Consul in Paris, Cobden says : " If you should be too modest to communicate this information, let me do so for you in a line or two which may be handed to those gentlemen when you call, informing them that you as President of the Union and Emancipation Society of Manchester have done more than any other man in England to produce that reaction in public opinion in favour of the North which has had so salutary an effect on the tone of our parliamentary politicians."

This tribute was well deserved.   Cobden, Bright, and a handful of stalwart defenders of the North had been doing all they could in a House of Commons on the whole bitterly hostile, much more hostile, one thinks, than the Government, and without the Govern-

[1] Later the founder of the Cobden Club.

ment's sense of responsibility. Their advocacy could, however, do little to influence
public opinion outside the House, and without
some evidence of popular support outside,
it is difficult to influence the House of Commons itself. Members pay great deference
to the clearly expressed opinions of their
constituents, though naturally they cannot
divine opinions which have not found some
sort of public expression. Even the smallest
minority may become a great force if members
realise that there is great and growing popular
support behind it, but no task can be conceived more disheartening than to face for
long months a hostile majority in the House,
which is conscious that it is backed up by
public opinion. It is hence the business of
those who would influence British politics to
go straight to the people, to open a propaganda
of leaflets, pamphlets, and above all, public
meetings. In this way only can the arms of
the politician at the front be strengthened,
and final victory be assured.

This had been the method of the Anti-Corn
Law League, and this was the method now
adopted by Mr. Potter. It is interesting to
note the names of those who signed the
address given to Mr. Potter on the dissolution

of the Society in 1866. We learn from it how many of those already or later famous in the literature, science, and politics of the country had consistently supported the North. The names include those of John Stuart Mill, Thomas Hughes, Professors Cairnes, Nichol, Goldwin Smith, Beesley, Thorold Rogers, and Fawcett, Hon. and Rev. Baptist Noel, Rev. Leslie Stephen, Messrs. Robertson Gladstone, Edward Dicey, F. J. Furnivall, and Frederic Harrison, besides many other men of mark in London and the provinces.

Perhaps the final Report presented to the Society on January 22nd, 1866, will give the best idea possible of its work and that formed by its members of its value.

" The Executive of the Union and Emancipation Society, in presenting their final Report, congratulate the members and friends of the Association on the auspicious termination of their labours.

" Five years ago a section of the United States of America, then known as the Slave States, sought by revolt and armed force the disruption of the Republic, and declared an intention to establish a Confederacy, whose corner stone should be Slavery.

" To aid in the accomplishment of this

gigantic crime societies were established in this country; and the Press, the platform and the pulpit became to a very large extent sympathetic with the wicked enterprise. The aristocracy, the gentry, and the commercial classes (with many noble individual exceptions), were dragging the nation into a partisanship with rebellion and slavery.

" At this critical period the Union and Emancipation Society was organised; ' to give expression, on behalf of the population of this district, to their earnest sympathy with the cause of Freedom, and fraternal regard towards their kinsmen of the United States; and to resist all recognition of the Slaveholding Confederacy.'

" The inaugural address of the Society soon elicited an approving response, both in this country and in the colonies. Adhesions were enrolled of representative men, eminent in thought and action, from all parts of the kingdom, along with many thousands of the industrial classes.

" The Executive disseminated, by means of the Press and the platform, the most accurate information upon the political and social history of the United States; the powers of the individual States; the prerogatives of the Federal Government; and particularly as to the causes and objects of the Rebellion.

" It was soon demonstrated that the *people* were emphatically true to their ancient love of freedom and constitutional government, and that the heart of England was sound on this great question.

" Although the contest here, against the manifold agencies of the Slave Power, was severe and varying, ultimately the conscience and common sense of the people triumphed, in and out of Parliament, and the public mind became steadfast in favour of the policy of neutrality and non-recognition, and confirmed in the belief that slavery was doomed.

" The progress of the conflict on the other side of the Atlantic, between the friends and foes of human liberty was watched by the Executive with deepening interest, but with unwavering confidence in the final triumph of freedom and civilisation.

" Early in the year 1865 came the collapse and downfall of the Slaveholders' Confederacy.

" In the first year of peace, ere the nation had ceased to mourn the loss of thousands of her bravest sons, and the death of her Martyr-President, Abraham Lincoln, the people of the United States amended the Federal Constitution—abolishing and for ever prohibiting Slavery throughout their great Republic.

" By this act millions of our fellow-creatures emerged from the condition of chattelhood into the higher region of manhood ; the stain which had disfigured the national flag of the United States was removed ; all her fruitful lands were opened to the civilising and ennobling influences of free labour; and the blessings of free schools, a free Press, and free government were secured as an inheritance for ever.

" The United States have thus proved to the world that ' a government of the people, by the people, for the people,' is competent to organise and wield vast combinations of power; to administer resources of extraordinary magnitude; to carry out the highest purposes of statesmanship to their most successful issues; and in the hour of triumph can exhibit a moderation of spirit and clemency towards the vanquished unexampled in history.

" The spectacle of hundreds of thousands of patriot soldiers returning to their peaceful callings and the duties of citizenship, is another suggestive lesson to the unenfranchised peoples, taxed to support the military monarchies of Europe.

" We commend to the benevolent consideration of our countrymen the claims of the freed men of the United States, whose sufferings, in their transition from bondage to liberty, appeal to the generous instincts of our common humanity.   We also especially urge the claims of the still-oppressed freed people in some of our own colonies, for the well-being of whom we are more directly responsible; and whose wretched condition calls for a practical manifestation of our Christian sympathy.

" In conclusion, we offer our congratula-
tions to our transatlantic friends, on the
restoration of peace, the preservation of the
Union, and the emancipation of the slave;
and whilst not unmindful of the difficulties
that surround their President, we recognise
his patriotism, moral courage, and practical
statesmanship, and record our earnest hope
that in the discharge of the functions of his
high office, he will secure beyond compromise
all the rights and privileges of citizenship to
his countrymen, without distinction of colour."

A note appended to the Report gives a
summary of the activities of the Society.
" Your Committee," it says, " have issued and
circulated upwards of *four hundred thousand*
books, pamphlets, and tracts, during the three
years of its operations; and nearly *five
hundred* official and public meetings have
been held in the promotion of the objects of
the Society." When we know that Mr.
Potter himself spent some £6,000 on behalf
of the Society, at a time when the cotton
famine was pressing the Lancashire business
men very hard, we realise how earnest was
the feeling of him and his fellow-workers in
the cause.

Now that they had got an opening, the
Northern sympathisers in this country soon

made themselves felt. We learn from a letter of Mr. F. W. Chesson, father of one of the writers of this book, and the Secretary for the London Emancipation Society, writing at the time (January 9th, 1863) that Professor Cairns's book on the *Slave Power : Its Character, Career, and Probable Designs* could not be obtained at Mudie's, though they had a large number of copies, so great was the demand for the book. Mrs. Stowe's address to the women of England had been printed entire in the *Morning Star* and *Daily News*. Chesson's testimony to the attitude of the working classes is strong and well deserved. They, he tells Garrison, " have proved to be sound to the core, whenever their opinion has been tested. Witness the noble demonstration of Manchester operatives the other day, when three thousand of these noble sons of labour (many of them actual sufferers from the cotton famine) adopted by acclamation an address to President Lincoln, sympathising with his proclamation. A friend of mine who was present on the occasion tells me that the heartiness and enthusiasm of the working men were something glorious; that he heard them say to one another that they would rather remain unemployed for twenty years than get cotton from the South at the expense of the Slave." [1]

There is a note of triumph, almost lyrical, in the letters of his friends to Garrison about this time. Thus George Thompson writes on February 5th, giving an account of his activities :—

"Since I last addressed you, I have attended meetings in the following places, viz. : Sheffield, Heywood, Dumfries, Kilmarnock, Greenock, Dumbarton, Paisley, Glasgow, Stirling, Perth, Aberdeen, Dundee, Edinburgh, Galashiels, Gloucester, Cheltenham, Bristol, Bath, Stroud, Kingswood, and London. The mention of some of these towns will bring old scenes to your remembrance, when we were companions and fellow-labourers—as, thank God, we still are. . . .

"Since I left Scotland, on the 22nd ultimo, my meetings have been all on the American question — and such meetings! They have reminded me of those I was wont to hold in 1831, '32 and '33—densely crowded, sublimely enthusiastic, and all but unanimous. The opposition has been of the most insignificant and contemptible kind. Before this reaches you, you will have seen the report of the meetings above and below, and in the

[1] *The Life and Times of William Lloyd Garrison,* vol. iv. p. 72.

open air around, Exeter Hall. I was the
same evening engaged in holding a meeting
at Stroud, which did not conclude till mid-
night. Three nights ago, I held a meeting
near my own residence. Thousands were
excluded for want of room. These outsiders
were addressed by competent persons, and
the cheers raised by the multitude found their
way into the meeting I was addressing, and
increased the excitement of my audience.
I shall rest till the 10th, and then recommence
my labours, which are in great demand.

*   *   *   *   *

" On New Year's Day, I addressed a
crowded assembly of unemployed operatives
in the town of Heywood, near Manchester,
and spoke to them for two hours about the
Slaveholders' Rebellion. They were united
and vociferous in the expression of their
willingness tu suffer all the hardships consequent upon a want of cotton, if thereby the
liberty of the victims of Southern despotism
might be promoted. All honour to the half
million of our working population in Lancashire, Cheshire, and elsewhere, who are
bearing with heroic fortitude the grievous
privations which your war has entailed upon
them ! The four millions of slaves in America
have no sincerer friends than these lean,
pale-faced, idle people, who are reconciled to
their meagre fare and desolate homes by the
thought that their trials are working out the
deliverance of the oppressed children of your

country. Their sublime resignation, their
self-forgetfulness, their observance of law,
their whole-souled love of the cause of human
freedom, their quick and clear perception
of the merits of the question between the
North and the South, their superiority to
the sophisms of those who would delude
them, and their appreciation of the labour
question involved in the 'irrepressible conflict,' are extorting the admiration of all
classes of the community, and are reading the
nation a valuable lesson."

It was the same everywhere. "On a Sun-
day," says Rhodes, *History of the United
States*, "Spurgeon thus prayed before his
congregation of many thousands : 'Now,
O God ! we turn our thoughts across the
sea to the terrible conflict of which we knew
not what to say ; but now the voice of freedom
shows where is right. We pray Thee, give
success to this glorious proclamation of
liberty which comes to us from across the
waters. We much feared that our brethren
were not in earnest, and would not come
to this. Bondage and the lash can claim no
sympathy from us. *God bless and strengthen
the North ; give victory to their arms !* ' The
immense congregation responded to this
invocation in the midst of the prayer with a
fervent amen."

When the British Government met to

prepare for the session of 1863, they had to confront a new element in any deliberations they might hold on the subject of the American Civil War. Hitherto, it had been possible to leave the British democracy out of account, or if its opinion was considered at all, to speculate and argue what that opinion might be. But the enthusiasm evoked by the President's proclamation ended all speculation on the subject. The opinion of the democracy was known and was, henceforth, a thing to be reckoned with in all future plans and policies. It would no longer be safe for the Chancellor of the Exchequer to talk about Jefferson Davis having "made a nation"; the British democracy was out to unmake slavery, and at least was determined to do nothing to hinder its destruction.

CHAPTER V

GETTYSBURG AND THE LAIRD RAMS

THE year 1863 was one of progress for the Northern cause. It began with a rapid growth in the sympathy felt for it on this side of the Atlantic; while during its course the military position altered so completely that the ultimate success of the North, apparently nearly hopeless at the end of 1862, seemed assured a year after.

It would seem that in France, even more than in the United Kingdom, the Government had all along misrepresented the feeling of the people. Unfortunately, it was Imperial not Republican France that was confronted with the problem of the American Civil War, a France in which freedom of the Press and of speech was not possible. An Empire, born in treachery, was destined soon after to fall in ruin, and was probably never representative of French opinion. Of this

we have evidence at the very commencement of 1864. " Your appreciation," says
Benjamin, " the Foreign Minister of the
South," writing to Henry Hotze, on January
9th, " of the tone and temper of public
opinion in France . . . concurs entirely in
the conclusion to which I have arrived from
the perusal of the principal organs of French
journalism. It has been impossible to remain blind to the evidence of the articles
which emanate from the best-known names
in French literature. In what is perhaps the
most powerful and influential of the French
periodicals, *La Revue des Deux Mondes*, there
is scarcely any article signed by the members
of its able corps of contributors which does
not contain some disparaging allusion to the
South. Abolition sentiments are quietly
assumed as philosophical axioms too self-
evident to require comment or elaboration,
and the result of this struggle is in all cases
treated as a foregone conclusion, as nothing within the range of possibility except
the subjugation of the South and the
emancipation of the whole body of the
negroes."

From the outset of the year the agents of
the South in Europe were beginning to find

themselves in difficulties. Slavery, the continuance and progress of which was the real object of the rebellion, was a skeleton in the cupboard which they were compelled as far as possible to hide even from those who sympathised most ardently with the South. Mason and Slidell, the representatives of the Confederate States in London and Paris, were themselves bigoted advocates of slavery, and long before the Secession War had been militant and unscrupulous pro-slavery politicians. They found here, however, that whatever sympathy they might win for disunion, they could get none for slavery. " They depended," says Mr. Bigelow, " for the success of their revolt, as they confessed, upon the sympathy and co-operation of two principal European States, in neither of which could be found a single statesman who would have dared to speak of slavery in any public assembly except in terms of abhorrence." Thinking, as they did, that negro slavery is a beneficent institution to be encouraged and extended wherever possible, it must have been a very difficult task for them to keep the family skeleton securely locked in its cupboard. Certainly, their English friends at least were incredibly simple, or it would have been impossible to conceal from them the fact that they were being used as tools by a gang of slaveholders.

Two amusing illustrations of the hidden conflict between pro-Southern Englishmen and their friends in America may be noticed. Mr. James Spence, a Liverpool gentleman, was an ardent admirer of the South, and had evidently come to be regarded as a sort of agent for the Confederate Government here. He had written a book, *The American Union*, in which, I presume, he endeavoured to prove the South in the right. How far he was successful in that may be doubted, but he certainly succeeded in proving that he did not understand the subject. Certainly, he gave high offence to his Southern friends by a paragraph in which he expressed his opinion of slavery. "In fact," he says, "slavery, like other wrongs, re-acts on the wrongdoer. Taking the most temperate view of it, stripping away all exaggerations, it remains an evil in an economical sense, a wrong to humanity in a moral one. It is a gross anachronism, a thing of two thousand years ago; the brute force of dark ages obtruding into the midst of the nineteenth century;

a remnant of elder dispensations whose harsh
spirit was law, in conflict with the genius of
Christianity, whose mild spirit is love. No
reasoning, no statistics, no profit, no philosophy can reconcile us to that which our instinct
repels. After all the arguments have been
poured into the ear there is something in the
heart that spurns them. We make no declaration that all men are born equal, but a
conviction—innate, irresistible—tells us, with
a voice we cannot stifle, that a man is a man,
and not a chattel. Remove from slavery, as
it is well to do, all romance and exaggeration,
in order that we may deal with it wisely and
calmly, it remains a foul blot, from which
all must desire to purge the annals of the
age." It was clearly seen at Richmond
that it would never do to have a gentleman
holding such views representing himself as
in any way officially connected with the
Confederate Government. Mr. Benjamin,
therefore, wrote to Spence, politely telling
him that the South had no further need for
his services. He was willing that Mr. Spence
should continue to enlist sympathy wherever
he could do so by imposing on others the
same mischievous delusion under which he
suffered himself, but the South would have

nothing to do with his heretical opinions. "It is quite probable," says Mr. Benjamin, "that the fact of your entertaining the opinions which you profess renders your advocacy of our cause more effective with a people whose views coincide with yours, and it would be folly on our part to reject the aid or alienate the feelings of those who, while friendly to our cause, are opposed to the institutions established among us. On the other hand, it appears to me that candour requires on your part the concession that no Government could justify itself before the people whose servant it is, if it selected as exponents of its views and opinions those who entertain sentiments decidedly averse to an institution which both the Government and the people maintain as essential to their well-being. The question of slavery is one in which all the most important interests of our people are involved, and they have the right to expect that their Government, in the selection of the agents engaged in its service, should refuse to retain those who are in avowed and public opposition to their opinions and feelings. I answer your appeal, therefore, by saying that, ' as a man of the world,' I would meet you on the most cordial terms without the slightest reference to your views on this subject; but that, 'as a member of a Government,' it would be impossible for me to engage you in its service after the publication of your opinions." [1]

At an earlier date the Southern envoys had come face to face with the utter detestation of slavery on the part of their most vociferous friends on this side the Atlantic. In November 1862 Mason wrote to his chief in Richmond describing an illuminating conversation he had recently had with a leading British Tory. "Some few days since," he says, "I dined with Lord Donoughmore, who was President of the Board of Trade during the late Derby Administration, and will hold the same, or a higher office, should that party again come into power: a very intelligent gentleman, and a warm and earnest friend of the South. In the course of conversation, after dinner, the subject came up incidentally, while we were alone, and he said I might be satisfied that Lord Palmerston would not enter into a treaty with us, unless we agreed in such treaty not to permit

[1] *Retrospections of an Active Life*, by John Bigelow, vol. ii. p. 126.

the African Slave Trade. I expressed my surprise at it, referring to the fact, that we had voluntarily admitted that prohibition into the Constitution of the Confederate States, thereby taking stronger ground against the slave trade than had ever been taken by the United States, that in the latter it was only prohibited by law; whilst in the former, not only was the power withheld from Congress, but the Legislative branch of the Government was required to pass such laws as would effectually prevent it.

" He said that was all well understood, but that such was the sentiment of England on this subject, that no Minister could hold his place for a day, who should negotiate a Treaty with any power not containing such a clause; nor could any House of Commons be found, which would sustain a Minister thus delinquent, *and he referred to the fact* (as he alleged it to be) *that in every existing Treaty with England that prohibition was contained.* He said further that he did not mean to express his individual opinion, but that he was equally satisfied, should the Palmerston Ministry go out, and the Tories come in, such would likewise be their necessary policy; and he added that he was well assured that England and France would be in accord on that subject." [1]

This caused a good deal of perturbation among the Southern leaders. They argued that the nature of their Constitution prohibited the re-introduction of the slave trade, and that any special clause in a commercial treaty compelling them to forbid it would be a reflection on their good faith. " If," said Mr. Benjamin, " the British Government would persist in the views you attribute to it, the matter can plainly be disposed of to much more advantage on this side of the water, and it may very well happen that that haughty Government will find to its surprise that it needs a treaty of commerce with us more than we need it with Great Britain."

While this rift was widening between the Southern rebels and their European friends, circumstances were steadily tending to hearten and unite the friends of the North. We soon get evidence of the effect produced by the British anti-slavery meetings which welcomed Lincoln's proclamation. Mr. Bigelow was then in Paris as Consul-General of

[1] *Retrospections of an Active Life*, by John Bigelow, vol. i. p. 566–567.

the United States, and even there he found evidence of the influence they exerted. Writing to Mr. Seward, February 6th, 1863, he says :—

" The anti-slavery meetings in England are having their effect upon the Government already. I enclose an evidence. The conductor of *Galignani*, Mr. Bowes, who was brought to my office one day last summer by Thackeray and to whom I have occasionally sent articles for publication, called recently, and not finding me, sent a letter which you will find enclosed. That paper always follows the Government, and hitherto, in spite of the social relations between Bowes and myself, has been exceedingly cruel on the North. The present advance on his part, therefore, is not without a significance. The Paris correspondent of the *London Post* also came to my house on Wednesday evening evidently disposed to be instructed. He says these intrigues in England merely express the public sentiment of the mass of English people—that there are about a dozen persons who by their position and influence over the organs of public opinion have produced all the bad feeling and treacherous conduct of England towards America. They are people who, as members of the Government in times past, have been bullied by the U.S. and compelled to submit to humiliation. They

know our strength and thought our statesmen used it brutally; they are not entirely
ignorant that the class who are now trying
to overthrow the Government were mainly
responsible for that brutality, but they think
we are as a nation disposed to bully, and
they are disposed to assist in any policy that
may dismember and weaken us. These scars
of wounded pride, however, have been care-
fully concealed from the public, who therefore cannot now be readily made to see why,
when the President had distinctly made
the issue between slave labour and free
labour, that England should not go with
the North. He says these dozen people
who rule England hate us cordially, that he
knows.

" I confess, bad as things look at home, I
derive great encouragement from the recent
popular demonstrations in England. When
Louis Napoleon found the Derby Ministry
intriguing with Austria and dynastic Europe
against him, he struck an alliance with the
people through Cobden and Derby. His
Commercial Treaty Negotiations made Cobden a power in England, and for the first
time, I believe, in her history England sent
a commoner as a plenipotentiary to France
and called two radicals into the Ministry.
Cobden did not lose his power until Napoleon
had entirely disarmed his enemies in England
and had placed the actual Ministry in a
position where he could unhorse it at a

moment's notice. We ought to take a leaf from the Emperor's book. We should strive to strike an alliance with the masses of Great Britain, and I have imagined the path was being smoothed for it by this popular movement against slavery : one of those issues which serve admirably as a means of organising the people and preparing them for more specific action when properly led. A good leader of the anti-slavery party there may soon hold the balance of power between two great parties. Is there nothing you can do : nothing the President or Congress can do to foster this organisation and direct it to good ends ? "

I think the correspondent of the *Post* took much too favourable a view of things. There were certainly far more than a dozen people at the back of the pro-South agitation in England, and the mischief was not confined to those who had immediate contact with American spread-eagleism. There was, nevertheless, a good deal of truth in this view, and it would be well if Americans realised how much this country was misrepresented by a minority during their troubles.

The community of language that unites

the British and American peoples, combined with certain consequences of their common origin, has for long kept up between them certain forms of intercourse impossible to anything like so great an extent between most other nations geographically far nearer to one another. The books and magazines of either nation enjoy a circulation in the other far beyond what would be possible but for the community of language, while speakers and lecturers on all subjects of common interest can find on either side of the Atlantic audiences equally numerous and equally interested. This is trite enough; it is perhaps less trite, though equally true, that there is an exceptionally large number of subjects of common interest to the two peoples. The Americans and English are nearer to one another in religion and moral outlook generally than either of them is to any other nation. There is a religious unity of the peoples, arising from the fact that there is the same diversity of religions in both. The Churches of England are all represented in America, as they are represented in no other foreign country in the world, while, with few exceptions, all but the newest of American Churches are represented here. It is the same with the great semi-religious causes which have their roots in the common puritanism of the race, of which the teetotal movement is the most typical. Even in matters less strictly moral or religious, the same common feeling asserts itself; if not in the programmes of social and political agitators, at least in their accent.

If, then, England has stood for Protestantism and dissent, America, as Burke said, has stood for the "dissidence of dissent and the Protestantism of the Protestant religion." And the community of language rendering this easy, no sooner has some new idea, religious, ethical, or social, got a foothold on one side of the water than some eloquent missionary transports it to the other. It would be a curious task to gather together the names of various lecturers who have, at one time or other, crossed the Atlantic to give their cousins the benefit of their inspiration. Dickens and Thackeray, Matthew Arnold and Emerson would figure along with the Booths, of the Blue Ribbon and Salvation Armies respectively, of Henry George, of J. B. Gough, of Moody and Sankey, and of Messrs. Torrey and Alexander, as well as of those with whom we are more particularly concerned here—Goldwin Smith and Henry Ward Beecher.

During the course of the war these eminent men from the two countries crossed the Atlantic, and did something to clear up the misunderstandings that had arisen between the nations. Beecher's tour in England and Scotland took place in the autumn of 1863, when he addressed eight mass meetings arranged by the Committee of Union and Emancipation in London, Liverpool, Manchester, Glasgow, and Edinburgh. In all his meetings, except the first at Liverpool, he had a most enthusiastic reception. Enormous audiences listened to him, while thousands of people were turned away from the doors through lack of room. In a letter written on the occasion of Goldwin Smith's reception in New York, he gave an illuminating account of the impression made on him by the tour.

" My own feelings and judgment underwent a great change while I was in England. Coming from home aglow with patriotic enthusiasm, I was chilled and shocked at the coldness toward the North which I everywhere met, and the sympathetic prejudices in favour of the South. And yet, everybody was alike condemning slavery and praising liberty !

" I soon perceived my first error was in supposing that Great Britain was an impartial spectator.   In fact, she was morally an actor in the conflict.   Such were the antagonistic influences at work in her own midst, and the division of parties, that, in judging American affairs she could not help lending sanction to one or the other side of her own internal conflicts.   England was not, then, a judge, sitting calmly on the bench to decide without bias ; the case brought before her was her own, in principle, and in interest.   In taking sides with the North, the common people of Great Britain and the labouring class took sides with themselves in their struggle for reformation ; while the wealthy and the privileged classes found a reason in their own political parties and philosophies why they should not be too eager for the legiti-mate government and nation of the United States.

" All classes who, at home, were seeking the elevation and political enfranchisement of the common people, were with us.   All who studied the preservation of the State in its present unequal distribution of political privileges, sided with that section in America that were doing the same thing.

" We ought not to be surprised nor angry that men should maintain aristocratic doc-trines which they believe in fully as sincerely, and more consistently, than we, or many among us do, in democratic doctrines.

" We of all people ought to understand how a government can be cold or semi-hostile, while the people are friendly to us. For thirty years the American Government, in the hands, or under the influence of Southern statesmen, has been in a threatening attitude to Europe, and actually in disgraceful conflict with all the weak neighbouring Powers. Texas, Mexico, Central America and Cuba are witnesses. Yet the great body of our people in the Middle and Northern States were strongly opposed to all such tendencies."[1]

In his short visit, it is clear Mr. Beecher had penetrated to the roots of British feeling in the matter. The struggle here, just as in America, was at bottom one between democracy and the classes. " During my visit to England," he said, when addressing an Abolitionist meeting on his return, " it was my privilege to address, in various places, very large audiences, and I never made mention of the names of any of those whom you most revere and love, without calling down the wildest demonstrations of popular enthusiasm, I never mentioned the name of Mr. Phillips,

[1] *A Welcome to Goldwin Smith by Citizens of New York*, Baker & Godwin, New York, 1864.

or Mr. Garrison, that it did not call forth a storm of approbation. It pleased me to know that those who were least favoured in our own country were so well known in England. . . . It is true that a man is not without honour save in his own country; and I felt that I had never had before me, in an audience here, such an appreciation of the names of our early and faithful labourers in this cause as there was in that remote country, among comparative strangers."

Goldwin Smith's visit to America, though it did not take place till the following year, may perhaps be mentioned here. He visited the States in 1864, mainly to see and report upon the Presidential election of that year. Goldwin Smith, however, had made himself so prominent by his consistent advocacy of the Northern cause that he had a warm welcome in the North. He bears emphatic testimony to the temper of the American people, thus called upon to elect their chief magistrate in the midst of the greatest civil war ever waged. "I came," he says, "to see a great political crisis. Would that all those who love, and all those who mistrust free institutions, could have seen it also! Would that they could have witnessed as I have the majestic calmness with which, under circumstances the most perilous and exciting, the national decision has been pronounced. Here is no anarchy, no military dictatorship. In the midst of civil war, a civilian is re-elected as President, by a constitutional process as tranquil as an English Sabbath day. And no king is more secure in the allegiance of his subjects than is the President in the allegiance of all—even those who voted against him—beneath his elective rule."

The valuable means of correcting false impressions rendered possible by the community of language and of moral outlook between the peoples, was not, I think, adequately used during the war. Bright and Cobden, it is true, kept up a regular correspondence with Sumner, and ardent Abolitionists, like George Thompson on this side, kept duly in touch with men of similar ideas, like Garrison, on the other, while we have some visits like those of Beecher and Goldwin Smith. Similar visits, however, carried out earlier in the war, might have done much to check the steady stream of vituperation that went on in the pro-Southern Press in England much earlier, and to counteract its mischievous influence in the States by persuading the American people that in Smith's own words, "the malignity which finds its organ in the *London Times* was that of a party, and not of the English people."

For the method thus employed of bringing the democracies face to face was eminently successful wherever it was employed, and contrasted strongly with the operations the Southern envoys were, during this year, carrying on in England and France. One is inclined to regret that neither Palmerston nor Russell had it in him to take the strong line President Wilson adopted under somewhat similar circumstances while yet America was a neutral in the late war. The attempt of the Austrian Ambassador and of the military representatives at the German Embassy to compromise the neutrality of the United States were met, as all the world knows, by expulsion from the country. Though this country was right enough in insisting on the envoys captured on the *Trent* being given up and allowed to proceed to Europe, it seems equally true that these gentlemen should have been promptly expelled from England and France as soon as they began to show what use they intended to make of their liberty.

Mason, the agent in England, it is true, did not do much mischief, probably because Mr. Mason appears to have been a fool, but Slidell, the accredited agent to France, was as astute and unscrupulous an intriguer as ever existed. His presence in Europe was a standing menace to the neutrality of France and incidentally of this country also. Captain Bullock, too, the naval agent of the Confederacy in England, was a very dangerous man. His energy had already got us into trouble by causing the *Alabama* and other cruisers to be built and launched under the very noses of the Government, and he was now superintending the building at Liverpool of two ironclad rams for the use of the Confederacy. Looking back at his activities from this distance of time, it would be hypocritical to blame Mr. Slidell for the methods he employed. His fundamental fault lay in the fact that his cause was a bad one; the methods he employed were imposed on him by the fact that it was not only bad but weak. But a nation or a cause desperately fighting for its life will naturally care very little for the convenience of neutrals or for diplomatic propriety. If it can compel the reluctant non-combatant to lend assistance, it will naturally do so: and if the neutral Power so used becomes so compromised with the enemy that it is ultimately forced to become an ally of the intriguing Power so much the better. It was clearly no part of Mr. Slidell's business to keep France or us on good terms with the United States; on the contrary, he had every reason to try to embroil us with them. It was our business and that of the Emperor of the French to watch all his proceedings with a vigilant eye, and if he showed the slightest disposition to push us out of the neutral course we had mapped out for ourselves, to expel him from Europe. That he played his part infinitely better than we did ours must frankly be conceded. That neither France nor England were thrown into war with the United States was no fault of his.

Mr. Slidell, though accredited to France, began operations by making two English members of the House of Commons, Messrs. Roebuck and Lindsay, his humble tools. As neither of these gentlemen ever showed any sympathy with slavery, this, in itself, must have been a fairly difficult thing to do. We have already seen how he made use of Lindsay in endeavouring to get the Emperor of the French and the British Government to break the blockade. In the spring of 1863, he made another attempt, and arranged an interview with Napoleon III for the two Englishmen to prepare the way for a motion which Roebuck was to introduce into the House of Commons. What passed at the interview in question is not quite clear, for the Emperor subsequently denied the truth of Roebuck's account of it. On June 30th, Roebuck introduced into the House of Commons a motion asking the Government " to enter into negotiations with the Great Powers of Europe for the purpose of obtaining their co-operation in the recognition " of the South. Great hopes had been entertained of the success of this motion; never was there a more dismal failure. The occasion was seized by Mr. Bright to make one of the most effective speeches he ever delivered. Employing all his powers of sarcasm and eloquence, Bright tore Roebuck's case to pieces, and the resolution which had been expected to pass the House by a large majority was ultimately withdrawn.

No doubt the credit for this is mainly due to Bright, but something, I think, must be allowed, even here, for the perception now borne in upon the House of Commons of the feeling outside parliament. The motion was tabled almost on the eve of the two most important victories of the North, Gettysburg and Vicksburg, victories which ultimately proved decisive. But though the tide was so near the turning, there was little at the moment to encourage the supporters of the North. Except in so far as the flight of time since then may have impressed people with the determination of the North to carry on the war to the bitter end, those who had for so long believed in the ultimate success of the South had little ground for changing their opinions of a year ago. The military position, then, could not influence the House of Commons, while individually the sympathies of members can hardly have changed. The influence of outside opinion, always respected by the House of Commons when clearly shown, was probably beginning to tell. It had become abundantly clear that the masses in England and Scotland were on the side of the North, that any intervention in favour of the rebellion would be resented by the people.

By one of Slidell's letters to Benjamin we know that he had been the means of obtaining the interview for Roebuck and Lindsay with the French Emperor, and it seems quite clear that it was he who arranged for Roebuck's

motion. We thus find a Southern agent
using two members of the British House of
Commons to bring in a motion helpful to his
own side and highly likely to entail grave
consequences for us, and arranging an interview for the same two members with the ruler
of a foreign Power in order to enable him to
disturb the policy of a British Cabinet, and
make use of our navy to further the designs
of the Confederate States and incidentally of
France !

Fortunately, the whole project failed, but
this was not the only attempt of Mr. Slidell to
use us for the benefit of the South. Lord
Russell was very angry at the way he had
been tricked over the *Alabama,* and was firmly
resolved to allow no more Southern cruisers
to leave our ports if he could help it. Two
vessels of a much more formidable type than
any yet launched were even then on the stocks
at Laird's, and were being built for the order
of the South. It became clear to the Southern
agents that these would not be allowed to leave
England unless some extraordinary means
were adopted to conceal their destination.
We learn from Mr. C. F. Adams, junior, what
these methods were. Slidell seems to have
managed to transfer the order to Bravay

and Co., a French firm, who were understood to require them for the Egyptian or some other foreign Government. At the same time the Confederates were having a fleet built for them in France. A licence to build and equip four ships had been obtained from the French Government under cover of a statement that they were " destined by a foreign shipper to ply the Chinese and Pacific seas between China, Japan, and San Francisco," and in addition to these two smaller ships and a gunboat were ordered. As armoured ships were then a novelty, and these vessels were to be added to the two armoured rams building in Liverpool, it seems clear that if once they had been delivered to the Confederates the blockade of the South would have been effectively broken. This would have given the South the one real chance left to it of victory. This will appear later; for the present it is only necessary to note that Slidell was deliberately trying to hoodwink both the French and British Governments. Neither of the Governments wished to allow their shipyards to be used for the purpose of building Confederate cruisers, ours, at least, was very angry at having been already once tricked over the *Alabama*. The real destination of the ships was therefore concealed by the impudent pretence that they were being built for neutral owners. It is useless to blame Slidell for this. As has been already shown, a nation fighting for its life will try every artifice to gain a point, and cannot be expected to care very much for the wishes or convenience of neutrals. It was for the French and British Governments to take care that he did not play fast and lose with their neutrality.

Very soon after the Roebuck abortive attempt to get us to interfere in the Civil War, the long-delayed crisis in the war itself had come. The war presents a certain rough but interesting likeness to the greater one just finished. As in the conflict of 1914–18 there was a main battle front in the Civil War, where, till almost the very end, no great territorial gains were made on one side or the other. This was the battle line between the Southern capital at Richmond and that of the United States at Washington. Here Lee confronted, and, till the last days of the war, held in check, the main armies of the North. From time to time, one side or the other would attack, endeavouring to break through and reach its enemy's capital, but though, owing to the less developed mechanism of war fifty years ago, the battles were shorter, the part played by this battle front resembles the fighting in France and Belgium sufficiently closely for all practical purposes.

If Lee could have commanded unlimited supplies and men, it is difficult to see why he ever should have been beaten. Whether he could do so or not, however, depended on the result of the struggle on other and subordinate battle-fields. While the fighting on the main front was going on, indecisively, but for a long time to the advantage of the South, the Federal armies gradually made themselves masters of the Mississippi valley, until only the fortress of Vicksburg remained to obstruct their control of the river. Meantime, the fleet blockaded the ports of the Southern States, until it should be possible to get possession of the coast and advance on the South from the rear. It is obvious that the victory of the North on these sides must ultimately render Lee's position untenable, unless he could break through and dictate peace at Washington before he became completely surrounded. Meantime, the operations of the American fleet present an obvious parallel to our blockade of Germany, and the movements in the earlier days of Grant on the Mississippi, and, later, the march of Sherman into Georgia, which ultimately gave the North command of the extreme South, present some resemblance to the various "side shows," which broke down the resistance of Germany's Allies.

In the beginning of July 1863 occurred two events impressive enough at the moment and ultimately decisive. After a terrible struggle, lasting three days, General Lee failed to force his way through the Federal army at Gettysburg on July 3rd, while on the following day Vicksburg, the last important fort on the Mississippi, was captured by General Grant. It was now clear, first, that the South were never likely to force their way to Washington and dictate peace there, and, secondly, that, however long it might take, sooner or later the Northern armies would occupy the country on Lee's rear and complete the defeat of the South. The only chance of preventing such an ending was to break the blockade and to open the way for supplies to come in from the sea. In fact, unless Slidell and his agents could succeed in tricking England or France into a virtual breach of neutrality, the cause of the South was hopeless.

Though, if Mr. Adams judged aright, the

first news of these victories tended to inflame rather than abate the eagerness of the reactionary forces in this country for intervention in the Civil War, responsible members of the Government must have regarded them in a very different light. The Confederate loan recently floated in England and France rapidly fell from 99 to 87, and continued to fall during the rest of the year. Ministers must have congratulated themselves on the failure of Mr. Roebuck's motion.

The rams were still being built at Laird's yard, however. Fine-sounding Eastern names had been given to them, *El Tousson* and *El Monassir*, to give colour to the idea that they were intended for the Egyptian Government, and also to throw difficulties in the way of Lord Russell in his efforts to detain them. To build warships for any foreign Government which may some day be at war with us is not a creditable way of making money, but it has, hitherto, been considered legitimate. By this means the leading industrial nations of the world have been able to reduce their natural superiority at sea in favour of pugnacious and less developed nations, like the Turks and the States of South America, to the profit of a few armament firms and to the general in-

crease of militarism throughout the world.
As long as this sort of trade is permitted,
however, it is a difficult thing for the Government
of a free country to interfere with
the delivery of any ships built by private
firms to their purchasers so long as the
Government for which they are intended is
actually at peace. If the destination of the
rams was that given out for them, Lord Russell
had only two alternatives before him—to let
the rams go, or to take them over by order
and add them to the British Navy. Without
producing a case and obtaining a vote in
parliament for such an increase in our ships,
this latter course might subject the Government
to severe criticism, and Lord Russell
seems to have found himself in a grave
difficulty. Behind the scenes was going on a
keen contest between Mr. Slidell, on the one
hand, and Mr. Adams in London, on the other;
the one trying to get delivery of the ships on
any pretext, the other to prevent them sailing.
The contest has been well described in the
biography of Mr. Adams, written by his son.
Slidell, fertile in expedients, and probably
realising that on his success in this matter
depended any possibility of victory for the
South, did his utmost, fortunately in vain.

We may pause at this point to examine what was implied by the release of Confederate cruisers from our ports. The *Alabama* and other Southern cruisers had all along occupied a very anomalous position in war. The Southern States, even at the outset, and much more from the time the Northern fleet had blockaded them, could not be a naval power at all, except by the assistance or connivance of some other State possessing open ports and coaling stations. The South was not an industrial nation like its rival, and if it were to have a navy at all the ships must be built abroad. Ranging the seas, as the *Alabama* did, its ships would, of course, have to call somewhere or other from time to time for coals and repairs, and naturally they would generally visit for these purposes the ports and stations of the maritime Empire whose dominions were scattered in all the seas of the world. In other words, the naval base of the Confederacy was not their own territory but the British Empire. Though, of course, the ships of the North enjoyed equally free access to our harbours, the aid thus afforded was no adequate offset to the assistance given to the South. The North had harbours of its own; it had men who could build ships and sailors who could man them, and stores of coal and munitions with which they could be supplied. British ports might be an assistance to the Northern navy, they were an essential to the very existence of that of the South.

The North had now got a stranglehold on its enemy, through the efficiency of the blockade and the victories of its armies, and nothing could in the long run save the South except the breaking of the blockade, and for that it must depend upon the willingness of Great Britain or France, or both combined, at least to supply her with a navy, at most to take up her quarrel. It was one of the great crises in the history of the world. If the two rams alone, not to speak of the fleet building in France, were released, the Northern blockade would almost certainly be broken, for the rams were then the most formidable vessels of war known. It is difficult to say what would have followed on the failure of the blockade so caused, but almost certainly it would have meant war between Great Britain, probably with France as an ally, and America. Under no circumstances could we have gained anything by this great catastrophe. Even if we won and the American Republic had been split in two, the Northern portion would still have been prospectively one of the greatest Powers in the world. Henceforth, too, it would have been a great military Power, fiercely anti-British in feeling. Now, the greatest guarantee for our hold on Canada, apart from the goodwill of the Canadian people themselves, is the non-military, non-aggressive character of the United States. If they were to strain their finances to support an enormous military establishment, they could keep a very much larger army on the St. Lawrence than ever we could muster there. I am convinced we could not possibly hold Canada against their will, and it seems pretty certain they would have wished to annex it if, through our action, they lost the rebellious States of the South. It is by no means certain, when we reflect on the enormous reserves of force in the Northern States and the difficulty of conducting a great war at such a distance from Europe, that the States, sorely pressed as they were, would not have won in the long run, and we might have lost Canada as an immediate consequence of the war. At any rate, we should have lost it ere now.

The French, having nothing to lose on the Continent, might have fared better, at least for a time. It would, no doubt, have been easy for Napoleon III to obtain a free hand in Mexico in return for his assistance against the North. It is not likely, however, that friendly relations would have lasted long if once the slave-owners had succeeded in forming their Republic. There was no slavery in Mexico, and French public feeling, quite as strong on this point as that of England, would certainly not have permitted its introduction. But the aggressive spirit of Southern slavery, always seeking by fair means or foul to extend the area of its peculiar institution, would not long have tolerated a free Mexico, either independent or under the virtual protection of France. Already, Texas had been torn from Mexico and annexed to the United States by the same people who were now in arms for secession. If the South had won, the rest of the unfortunate country would, we may be sure, ere long have shared the same fate.

Fortunately, these issues are merely speculative. Puzzled as he was by the devices of Mr. Slidell, Lord Russell was determined not to repeat his error of the *Alabama ;* the opinion of the British democracy was known by this time; the North were now steadily gaining the upper hand, and there seemed no likelihood that a Southern Republic would be established and claim recognition. Accordingly, on the 9th of September, an order was issued officially detaining the suspected ships, and in the following month they were seized by the Government. The effect was immediate. Confederate bonds fell from 79 to 65, an indication that the investing public, at least, realised the significance of the step taken. The chairman at Ward Beecher's first meeting in Manchester, amidst loud applause, read a telegram conveying the news. All danger of British interference in the American Civil War was at an end, and a way, however long, lay open to a full understanding between the English-speaking peoples.

CHAPTER VI

THE CLOSE OF THE WAR AND AFTER

THIS is, perhaps, the time to survey the permanent effect produced on the relations of the English-speaking peoples by the general attitude during the war of the Government of the United Kingdom. The war itself had now reached its concluding phase. With the victories at Gettysburg and Vicksburg, the chances of the South ultimately beating the North on the field were ended, and the detention of the Laird rams soon rendered it certain that the United States Government had no further reason to fear European intervention. The Federal troops had much hard fighting still before them, but even the worst checks they might have to sustain from this time forward could only serve to delay, not to prevent, an inevitable result. It is true there were still ships being built for the South in France, but it is clear that much as Napoleon III desired intervention in the conflict, he had never been willing to venture on such a step without the concurrence of Britain. Very soon after the Laird rams had been detained, the Southern agents began to find themselves in difficulties about the French ships.

Circumstances, too, were providing the Emperor with a very good excuse for getting out of an embarrassing position. It would seem that he had been willing enough to allow Confederate ships to be built in France, but would only guarantee to allow them to leave the country provided " their destination could be concealed." For this reason, as we have seen, Mr. Slidell had arranged an elaborate comedy, by which they were to leave France as if they were intended to cruise or trade in the Pacific. In September, a few weeks before the English rams were detained, however, the American Embassy in Paris was put in possession of convincing proofs that these ships were detained for the Confederacy. The action of the British Government may probably have had something to do with his attitude, but the Emperor seems to have been very glad to avail himself of the excuse. The Southern envoys soon found that they could neither get delivery of the ships then building for them, nor even obtain permission for

Southern cruisers which had called at French ports for repairs to leave again. Mr. Slidell was thus placed in a quandary, and on February 6th, 1864, he wrote to Richmond giving the following account of the position :—

" By referring to the report of my conversation with the Emperor contained in my No. 38, you will find that, while fully assenting to the arming and departure of the corvettes, he consented only to the building of ironclads for our account and did not commit himself to permit their sailing unless their destination could be concealed. This in the case of ironclads could only be done by setting up an apparent ownership by some foreign Government as to the corvettes. They were to be represented as intended for commercial purposes in the Indian Ocean, China, etc. The contract for the corvettes was concluded only after the official consent to their armament and sailing was given by the Minister of Marine, and this was given on the representation that they were intended for commercial purposes, although their real character and destination were fully known to him; he, however, reluctantly signed the order in obedience to superior authority. No such authority was given in the case of the ironclads, and *I was ignorant that any contract was in contemplation for their construction until after it had been made.* I mention these facts, not with the most remote idea of implying any censure upon Captain Bullock, but to establish the distinction to be drawn between the two classes of vessels, which is necessary to bear in mind in order to come to a proper decision as to the course to be pursued in relation to them. In the first interview I had with the Minister of Marine on the 19th November, consequent on my note to the Emperor of the 9th of November contained in my No. 48, he drew a very broad line of distinction between the corvettes and the ironclads, saying that with proper precautions the former might be permitted to go to sea, but that the ironclads being from their very build solely fitted for warlike purposes, their being permitted to sail in spite of the remonstrances of the Washington Government, and in violation of the Emperor's declaration of neutrality, *would be an overt act of hostility.*

" The question now presents itself, what is to be done with these vessels? M. Arman, the builder of these ironclads, was informed that they will not be permitted to go to sea except as the property of some non-belligerent Government; this was before the breaking-out of hostilities between Denmark, Austria, and Prussia. Captain Bullock, after consulting Mr. Mason, Commodore Barron and me, determined to sell the ironclads. They could have been disposed of, at a considerable advance on their cost, to Denmark or to Russia, but the pending war may put these purchasers as belligerents out of the market. Commodore Barron and Captain Bullock say that the corvettes were intended to act in conjunction with the ironclads in raising the blockade on our coasts, and this object being no longer attainable and there being few Federal merchant vessels afloat, they are disposed to sell the corvettes also, at least two of them. I do not agree with them in this view of the case. Should we withdraw our cruisers, the Federal flag would soon resume on the ocean the rank which we have forced it to abdicate; we cannot expect the *Alabama* and *Florida* always to avoid the pursuit of the enemy, and we should be prepared to supply their loss."

"Suffice it to say," wrote Mason, the Confederate agent in England, " the conviction has been forced upon us that there remains no chance or hope of getting ships from either England or France. . . . From England we have long since had nothing to expect; from France we have the right to entertain a belief of other results."

Another indication of the growing coolness of the French Government towards the cause of the South comes from the correspondence of Slidell. The unfortunate Archduke Maximilian was doubtful whether he should accept the Imperial Crown of Mexico offered to him by Napoleon, and in December 1863, as we learn from Slidell's correspondence, he actually stipulated that before he took any part in the matter the new Empire must be recognised by the Confederate States. So rapidly did the Confederates lose prestige in France, however, that in the following March we find the Archduke making excuses to avoid an interview which he had promised to Slidell. This and other evidences of coolness showed, as Slidell thought, the Emperor's " increased desire to avoid giving umbrage to the Lincoln Government." Not long after this the Emperor himself withdrew the promise of an interview he had given to Mr. Slidell, and though at a chance meeting months afterwards the Emperor was personally friendly, it seems evident that the French Government no longer intended to give the South even secret encouragement. The Southern Government felt the changed state of affairs very keenly and were very indignant with France. " It is unfortunately but too true," wrote Benjamin to Slidell, after giving a list of the sins of the French Government, " that this Government is not now in a position to resist such aggressions, and France is not the only nation which has unworthily availed itself of this fact, as the messages of the President have on more than one occasion demonstrated to the world. There is one contrast, however, between the conduct of the English and French Governments that does not redound to the credit of the latter. The English Government has scarcely disguised its hostility from the commencement of the struggle. It has professed a newly invented neutrality, which it has frankly defined as meaning a course of conduct more favourable to the stronger belligerent. The Emperor of the French professed an earnest sympathy for us, and a desire to serve us, which, however sincere at the time, have yielded to the first suggestion of advantage to be gained by rendering assistance to our enemy."

The truth seems to be that the Emperor was shrewd enough to see that interference in the Civil War would be dangerous, unless he could secure the co-operation of the British fleet, and that, it was now plain, he was not likely to have. This country, too, had from the first favoured the Monroe doctrine, and as long ago as the days of Canning had made it clear that we did not favour European armed intervention in American affairs. Louis Napoleon was not a favourite in England, there was always a danger that we might do more than merely refuse to co-operate with France if she interfered alone in the quarrel. Our refusal to release the Laird rams, then, should, I think, be counted to our credit by Americans, as at least an important step, not only in preserving our own neutrality, but indirectly in holding the French Emperor in check.

Throughout 1864 and the following spring the war gradually worked out to the now inevitable end, raising no new questions of importance in the relations of this country and America. It is a gallant story enough, the chief honours of which fall to the great President of the United States and to one of the noblest men who ever lent the glory of his name to a bad cause. One can understand, even without sharing the loyalty of the Cavalier or Jacobite; it is impossible at this day to surround with any halo of romance the cause of the Southern slave-owner. Such names as those of Falkland in England and Montrose in Scotland, though they do not depend for the honour we render to them on the lost cause for which they fought, nevertheless, lose nothing by association with it. Lee was the noblest of many brave men who

fought for a cause with which it is difficult to
have even a sentimental sympathy.   As he
seems to have disapproved of slavery and to
have been personally opposed to secession,
it is a little difficult to understand how he
came to fight on the side of the South at all.
He seems, however, to have had what I may
call a "soldier's conscience," and to have
believed that his first duty was not to consider the rights or wrongs of the quarrel, but
to fight for his State, and as Virginia wished
to secede, he conceived it his duty to help her
to do so.   This is an ethical position that will
not stand criticism.   It is not necessary,
however, to defend the doctrine of "my
country," in this case "my State, right or
wrong," to recognise the moral greatness of
General Lee.   We may reject his ideal, while
recognising the heroism of the man who fought
for it.   We can feel glad that he was fighting,
not for slavery, but for Virginia, and honour
him as one of the noblest men the United
States have produced.

The Southern agents in Europe were much
more truly representative of the cause for
which they worked so hard.   It is of some
importance to show how dissatisfied these men
were with their treatment here, as it may

serve to disabuse Americans of the idea that even official England was entirely pro-Southern. This country, indeed, was singularly unfortunate in its experiences during the Civil War. Perhaps we did not attempt to please either; certainly, we succeeded in bitterly offending both. It was as when Mr. Pickwick rushed between the angry editors and received the fire shovel on one side and the carpet bag on the other. Thus, while people on the Northern side were threatening eternal hatred of this country because of our conduct in the *Trent* affair, the correspondence between the Southern agents and the Government at Richmond contained such sentiments as the following :—

" Nothing can exceed the selfishness of English statesmen except their wretched hypocrisy, they are continually canting about their disinterestedness, magnanimity and abnegation of all other considerations than those dictated by a high-toned morality, while their active policy is marked by egotism and duplicity."—*Slidell to Benjamin, August 24th,* 1862.

" Your correspondence with Earl Russell shows with what scant courtesy you have been treated, and exhibits a marked contrast between the conduct of the English and French statesmen now in office in the intercourse with foreign agents eminently discreditable to the former. It is lamentable that at this late period of the nineteenth century a nation so enlightened as Great Britain should have failed to discover that a principal cause of dislike and hatred towards England, of which complaints are rife in her Parliament and in her Press, is the offensive arrogance of some of her public men."—*Benjamin to Mason, October 28th, 1862.*

" I fully appreciate the wisdom and prudence of your suggestions relative to the distinction which ought to be made by the Press and by our Government between the English Government and people. You will doubtless have observed that the President's message is careful (while exposing the duplicity and bad faith of the English cabinet, and Earl Russell's course of abject servility towards the stronger party and insulting arrogance towards the weaker) to show no feelings of resentment towards the English people. The sentiment of wrong and injustice done to us, of advantage meanly taken of our distress, of conduct towards our representative in London unworthy of a man possessing the instincts of a gentleman, all combine to produce an irritation which it is exceedingly difficult for the most temperate to restrain, and Earl Russell has earned an odium among our people so intense as to require the utmost caution on the part of those in authority to prevent its expression in a form that would be injurious to the public interests."—*Benjamin to Henry Hotze, January 9th, 1864.*

It cannot be said that the hostility of the South was quite devoid of justification. Their agents were treated with scant courtesy. Thus Cobden writes to Sumner : " If Lord Russell's despatches to Mr. Adams are not very civil, he may console himself that the Confederates are still worse treated."

It is a relief to turn from these expressions of animosity to the relations between the American democracy and those who from the first had been enthusiastically on their side. Nothing is more pleasing than the profound gratitude of the American people to Bright and Cobden. By it one sees what a great opportunity the statesmen of those days lost through lack of a similar whole-hearted sympathy with the North. All the bitter memories of the Civil War, all pleasure in "twisting the tail of the British lion," all hesitation in taking sides with us in any great struggle in which we might subsequently have been engaged, would have been for ever removed, if the attitude of these men had been that of the Government and the Press. In that case an Anglo-American entente, the desire for which is now felt by so many people on both sides of the Atlantic, would probably have been an immediate result of the Civil War.

Two striking incidents show how deeply the American people appreciated the work done for their cause by the two great Free Trade statesmen.   Mr. Bright had pleaded for a pardon to a British subject, Alfred Rubery, who had been convicted of a plot to seize a vessel in San Francisco harbour and to take it out as a privateer on the side of the South. When he heard that Bright had interceded for this man, Mr. Lincoln issued the following remarkable pardon, the terms of which are probably unique among similar documents :—

" Whereas one Alfred Rubery was convicted on or about the twelfth day of October 1863, in the Circuit Court of the United States for the District of California, of engaging in, and giving aid and comfort to the existing rebellion against the Government of this country, and sentenced to ten years' imprisonment, and to pay a fine of ten thousand dollars ;

" And whereas, the said Alfred Rubery is of the immature age of twenty years, and of highly respectable parentage ;

" And whereas, the said Alfred Rubery is a

subject of Great Britain, and his pardon is desired by John Bright, of England;

" Now, therefore, be it known that I, Abraham Lincoln, President of the United States of America, these and divers other considerations me thereunto moving, and especially as a public mark of the esteem held by the United States of America for the high character and steady friendship of the said John Bright, do hereby grant a pardon to the said Alfred Rubery, the same to begin and take effect on the twentieth day of January 1864, on condition that he leave the country within thirty days from and after that date."

As Lord Morley tells us, the names of Cobden and Bright were inscribed on tablets on two of the great trees of the Yosemite Valley. Of this striking manifestation of esteem, Cobden writes to his colleague : " I hope you were pleased with the compliment paid us in California. There is a poetical sublimity about the idea of associating our names with a tree 300 feet high and 60 feet girth ! Verily it is a monument not built with men's hands. If I were twenty years younger I would hope to look on these forest giants; great trees and rivers have an attraction for me."

Equally strong was the impression made on

the people of America by the patience of those
who suffered from the cotton famine in Lancashire.   It was Mr. Bright who suggested to
Sumner what an effect might be created in
England, if Americans would make some contribution to lessen the severity of the famine.
The hint was taken up and three vessels
loaded with barrels of flour were sent over from
New York to the Mersey.   In fact, Americans
were eager for British sympathy and were
grateful wherever they found it.   The pity is
that they got so little of it, or rather, perhaps,
that the very real and widespread sympathy
that existed among millions of British people
for their cause was so hidden by the vindictive
and foolish utterances of a noisy minority.

But the Government was in the hands of
men less wise than Cobden, less simple-
hearted than the Lancashire workers.   With
them it was not merely a question of liberty
or slavery, but a balance of complex motives
and interests very hard to adjust and necessarily shifting from day to day.   Horror of
the war itself and resentment at the economic
hardships it imposed on neutral countries
obscured for them the great human cause at
the bottom of it.   The Cabinet was divided
between those who sympathised, not very

ardently, with the North, and those who favoured, but without enthusiasm, the cause of the South. It is certain that Russell and Palmerston, at least, the two most powerful men in the Government, at one time actually contemplated recognising the South, and that when Gladstone made his unhappy Newcastle speech we were within an ace of doing so.[1] Something intervened, however, and almost immediately after the opinion of the British democracy became so unmistakable that the project was dismissed. But it was impossible for either side to feel cordial towards the British Government, which, on its part, felt no cordiality for either. Whatever, then, the masses of England may have felt, the close of the Civil War found England less popular both with North and South than she was at the beginning.

As the war drew to its close there is evidence of a changed spirit, even among those who had supported the South. We know from Lord Morley's biography how bitterly Gladstone regretted his offensive Newcastle speech, and his regret at a past error was probably shared by many thousands of less illustrious people.

[1] See Correspondence between Russell and Palmerston, Bigelow, vol. i. pp. 544, 550.

The war had barely ended, too, when a terrible event turned all eyes in sympathy to America. The assassination of President Lincoln, on April 14th, 1865, just after his installation for a second term of office after the triumph of the North, is one of the most dramatic events in history. Its practical consequences were doubtless grave enough, for it placed the supreme power in the hands of a man far inferior to the great leader, at the time when the wisest leadership was wanted in the work of reconciliation and reconstruction imposed on the Republic. To what extent the loss of his wise guidance affected the actual settlement must be always a matter of conjecture, but what is not conjectural at all is the effect his tragic death had on the moral judgment of the world on Lincoln's own career. For long he has been recognised as one of the greatest statesmen of the nineteenth century, and even had he come to a peaceful end this would have been realised ere now. The fame which the lapse of time would have earned for Lincoln in any case, the pistol of Booth secured for him in a moment. The fine verses in which *Punch* recanted all the unkind things it had said of him in the war, while uttering a glowing tribute to his character, were an index of a universal feeling. From the moment the news of his death came to this country, it is safe to say that with ninety-nine out of every hundred people in England Lincoln's memory stood with that of Washington as one of two great Americans who, whatever may have been said of them in their lives, were worthy of all honour in death. The *Punch* poem seems to have produced a striking effect in America, while the many other tributes to Lincoln's memory which came from all over the Old World must have done something to soothe the ruffled feelings of the people there.

There were, therefore, three beneficent influences at work during and after the Civil War to soften the resentment of Americans at our official attitude : the work of such leaders as Cobden, and Bright, and of such organisations as the Committee of Union and Emancipation; the sympathy of the working classes in Lancashire and elsewhere, in so far as this was realised in America; and the evidence of a complete revulsion of feeling even among former opponents which followed Lincoln's murder. Whether the protracted negotiations on the *Alabama* claims which followed shortly after the war tended on the whole in the same direction, it would perhaps be hard to say. The submission of these claims to an arbitration court and their peaceful settlement marks an important stage in international relations. On the whole it is creditable to both nations, and everybody will approve of the precedent then created. At the time, however, it may well have aroused as much feeling as it allayed. The Americans certainly considered that they had suffered a much greater amount of damage than that for which they received compensation, and would not be much conciliated by the scornful way in which their more extravagant claims were received. On the other hand, it cannot be denied that, having regard to the previous practice of powerful States and the false standard of honour generally accepted in international relations, it was a trying thing for a proud nation like Britain to submit to have its conduct reviewed and condemned by foreign judges. The nations, henceforth, were officially friends, and both Governments were anxious to keep them so, but the more militant citizens of both felt aggrieved until in a very few years the whole thing became forgotten.

If, as I believe, the net effect of the Civil War was to leave the feelings at least of the

Americans to us rather worse than it found them, the forces that were gradually tending to heal a yet older sore must have suffered interruption.   One sign of the growing desire on the part of Americans to promote friendly relations with this country is the movement now going on for the more impartial teaching of history in American schools.   The school histories of most lands are probably grossly partial, and it is not perhaps surprising that Englishmen who have been in the States complain bitterly of the way in which this country is treated in the history books used in American schools.   Whether they are on the whole worse in this respect than those of other countries, I am not prepared to say, but, at any rate, the sort of thing complained of is neither new nor peculiar to America. What *is* new is the honourable desire of the Americans to correct this fault and the strenuous efforts they are making to do so.   School text-books have been examined and classified according to the extent to which they are fair or unfair in their presentation of the relations between this country and the United States, and schoolmasters are advised to prefer the fairer and better type of text-book to the more one-sided histories which have

hitherto been used. A report issued by the
American Government proves that very considerable progress has been made in the
desired direction. The more recent books
issued to schools showed a marked improvement on the older ones, though there was
still great room for improvement.

Whether American school histories were
more partial than those of other nations or
not, it would not be easy to say without a
comparative study involving the school books
of many nations. It is clear, however, that
owing to the nature of the case, it is England
alone, or almost alone, that is the victim of
misrepresentation in this case, whereas in
most other countries anti-foreign feeling is
divided among many other nations. It is
mainly with Great Britain that the United
States have had critical relations, and it is
almost entirely over the revolutionary war
that American national enthusiasm can be
displayed. Thus, the instinct that leads
nations to train their youth in patriotism at
the expense of justice to other countries is
naturally in America more than elsewhere
a basis of Anglophobia. It was doubly
unfortunate that when the remains of anti-
British feeling had had nearly a century to die

out they should be revived by the new causes of friction introduced by our official attitude during the Civil War. The forces bringing the two peoples together, the community of language and ideas, the interchange of speakers, the common work on many issues of social and religious reform, constitute a slow but steady influence gradually dissolving the animosities of bygone times. In the long run, they must be much more potent, because constantly at work, than the passing waves of feeling, favourable or adverse, provoked by some incident of the day. Nevertheless, the friction engendered by the war gave a sad set-back to this healing influence, and it was not until the Americans found themselves strongly supported by us in the days of their war with Spain, that England became popular in the States. Indeed, the outburst of British sympathy seems to have surprised our American cousins, and did something to atone for our faults in the Civil War.

For the roots of Anglo-American friendship we must look back far into the past, before the days of the Pilgrim fathers, before Magna Carta, before even Hengist landed at Ebbs-

fleet.   They are to be found in the old liberty
of the Gothic tribes, transplanted beyond the
seas into regions where they could be developed apart from the conflicts and dangers of
feudal Europe.   Amid the strifes of the Continent, ordered liberty could only find a
precarious refuge among the cities of Italy, on
the mountains of Switzerland, or the half-
submerged lands of Holland.   In early times
the Channel was to us much what the Atlantic
is to our kinsmen; it gave us the opportunity
to develop the civilisation inherent in the old
Teutonic life without much interference from
the European Powers.   The notion that
Britain was another world, comparatively
speaking a *New* World, seems not to have
been unknown in Saxon times.   We were too
near the Continent and it must be frankly
admitted far too pugnacious to evolve a
Monroe doctrine for Great Britain, but we
were sharply enough divided from it to meddle
with Europe only when we wanted to do so,
and only to the extent which we desired.
It was not because we were instinctively more
devoted to freedom than other countries,
that we were always in practice more free,
that our feudalism was less arrogant, and our
monarchy, even at the height of its power,

more deferential to the people than those of the Bourbons or the Hapsburgs. On the Continent the primitive freedom became submerged in a flood of despotism, here it was always alive locally and never entirely forgotten nationally. Kings in England could always be popular and their commands always be loyally obeyed when the people were commanded to do what they liked. When, however, the people did not happen to have the same wishes as the King, the latter generally found things very uncomfortable. Magna Carta was probably merely a statement of what were conceived to be the inalienable rights of Englishmen. Few Englishmen have ever read it, yet it remained for centuries an object of almost superstitious reverence to the nation. This was because, if the Charter itself was but a name to most, its essential principles were understood and kept alive even in the worst of times. The people never lost the instinct of self-government, for they never entirely lost that which alone can keep it alive, the practice of it.

Thus, the earliest English colonists in America were a politically capable people, who were placing between them and European despotism not merely a narrow strait, but the wide Atlantic. Transferred to a new Continent, these English exiles were more an island people than ever, freer even than their forefathers or those they left behind to develop their native liberties in their own manner. Distance emphasised, it did not change their essential character. More logical than ours, their revolution, when it came, was still similar; it was self-centred, American, non-missionary and non-aggressive. It is this lack of missionary spirit, this insular character, that distinguishes the Anglo-Celtic revolutions from those of France and Russia. France would make Europe Jacobin; Russia would make the world Bolshevik; but though no doubt the later history of the world has been profoundly affected by what was done in England in the seventeenth and America in the eighteenth century, that is not because the authors of these revolutions sought to impose them on others, but simply because such striking events were sure sooner or later to provoke imitation elsewhere.

There is thus a conservative element even in the revolutions of the English-speaking peoples, arising out of the fact that they are only attempts to give a new security and a modern form to primitive freedom never

wholly lost. Over revolutionary debate the
spirit of Burke presides, imposing on enthusiasm the method of temperance and order.
And in both nations, especially in America,
there is a wonderful power of assimilation,
subduing to the temper of the race all alien
elements absorbed into it. This is due, perhaps, to the fact that in the whole white race
the same essential principles are inherent,
though on the Continent they have been over-
laid by centuries of feudalism and despotic
rule. Where the old ideas have been divided
by protecting seas from the discords of Europe,
they have survived and developed; where
despotism has cut asunder the knots which
bind men to the past, liberty could only revive
by being re-created from the base. But the
nations that have poured into America and
the British colonies are being re-grafted on
to their old stock, and at bottom the ideals
of the Anglo-Celtic race are not peculiar to it.
They are human, not merely English; they are
eternal, not modern.

Thus it comes about that, though not missionary in intention, and though slow in
operation, the ideals of the Anglo-Celtic
peoples have powerfully affected Europe, and
by all indications are likely to do so far more

in the future. While one country, almost alone, and that not the most powerful, stood for popular liberties, the great mass of Europe could be but slightly influenced. Authority everywhere stood enthroned; liberty seemed insignificant and discredited. Now, however, all this is reversed. More securely islanded by the ocean than ever England was by the strait, America and the Dominions have expanded till now together they represent the greatest power in the world. If they work together in harmony, nothing can long withstand the influence of their ideals. That this should be so, must be the hope of every one who wishes to see any return to the traditions of feudal and despotic Europe impossible.

B. V.

CHAPTER VII

VOICES OF THE 'SIXTIES

(By W. H. Chesson)

Mr. Brougham Villiers having narrated the story of Anglo-American friction during our Cousins' Civil War, the responsibility for a perfectly orderly statement rolls off him— but without embarrassing me, because my task is in the nature of an essay. Essay is a happy word for a nervous author's work if a critic is to peer at it, for there are fewer rules for essayists than even for experimenters!

As to the voices which speak in this chapter, I would there were more of them. That Disraeli is not overheard—for to overhear would have been even better than to hear him—depresses me. " What an uneasy-looking face he has ! How mysterious the expression, and how satirical the play of humour on the lips ! " remarks my father in his diary for July 11th, 1862, after seeing him roaming about the scenes of the International Exhibition ; and it would at least have served art if the Sphinx of Imperialism had said that of which the diarist could only see the token. Other silences besides Disraeli's are also conspicuous in this essay, notably that of my father's friend, Louis Alexis Chamerovzow, secretary of the Anti-Slavery Society, London, during the last years of slavery in the United States. For between an essayist and the conscientious historian there is as much difference in observance as between a ratepayer out for a stroll and the District Surveyor on duty. Diffidence having now uttered its not "inevitable" words, the better business of this essay begins.

.   .   .   .   .

Although it is wise to insist on the non-idealistic element in quarrel and umbrage, one cannot ignore the influence of American slavery on English opinion in the 'sixties. True, even to-day the vicious violence permitted by that institution is fatuously overlooked by those who, comparing a "skivvy" or a beggar, an unemployed or an over-employed freeman, with a slave of Jamaica or Georgia, inquire ironically, "What's in a name?" Ignorance, however, though it glories in feeling like an encyclopædia, is precisely as frail a thing as darkness. No one, confronted by the facts of slavery, the advertisements for escaped slaves, the architecture of the slave-ship, the mechanism of auctioneering, the hideous commercialism of the whipping-house, slavery's horrible carefulness (*e. g.* the formula for corporally chastising a pregnant woman), is unable to perceive the obstacle to the establishment of an intelligent cordiality between England and the American Republic in the earlier 'sixties.

That the *roman à clef*, or even fiction without a key, is a very powerful instrument in the formation of views no one will deny. The elder Dumas might even have persuaded us that Nero was as great an athlete and artist as he was a criminal, if it had not been that the death of his mother troubled his genius too much when he was writing *Acté*. Swinburne might turn his back on a "sable and servile hero" and dub Mrs. Stowe a "mænad of Massachusetts," but, nevertheless, *Uncle Tom's Cabin* produced much profoundly adverse sentiment against the United States, although the disguised helotry of our "hind-most" were arguments against British Phari-saism. A not too modest tribute to the qualities of "Uncle Tom" was paid in or about 1857 by a "Southern" judge who sentenced "Samuel Green, a respectable free colored man of Maryland, and a Methodist preacher, to ten years' imprisonment in the Penitentiary for having in his possession a copy of *Uncle Tom's Cabin*." (See *Annual Reports of the American Anti-Slavery Society*, New York, 1859.)

Mrs. Stowe's thrilling and thoroughly " documented " story seems to have crowded others out of the present public's memory; but R. Hildreth's *The White Slave* (1852), and the harrowing narrative *Clotel; or the President's Daughter*, by the " fugitive slave " William Wells Brown, which appeared in 1853, were probably alive in the popular mind when the American Civil War began to strain the velvet of our diplomacy. Moreover, in 1862 an extraordinarily interesting narrative of slavery, written by Mrs. Harriet Jacobs, an escaped slave, was launched in London through the efforts of my father. Entitled here *The Deeper Wrong*, and in the United States *Incidents in the Life of a Slave-girl*, it relates the experiences of a slave-mother, seduced by a white bachelor, though she rejected the amorous proposals of a cruel and married master. A long review of it by Mrs. Amelia A. E. Chesson appears in *The Morning Star* for March 10th, 1862. " The work is

edited," says the reviewer, "by Mrs. Lydia
Maria Child, an American authoress whose
delightful contributions to juvenile literature
[especially *The Girl's Own Book*] have been
read at almost every fireside where the Anglo-
Saxon tongue is spoken." On March 31st,
1862, my father records " the sorry news that
a cheap pirated edition of *The Deeper Wrong*
has been published. . . . How much we need
a copyright treaty with America ! "

Our language supplies a colloquialism for
humbling a swain too ambitious in love :
" she is meat for your master " : it is surely
one of those turns of speech to which the noun
" vulgarity " owes its implication of coarse-
ness ; but if we alter the phrase into " she is
meat for *her* master," vulgarity is worsened
into a crude hint of animalism. Often might
this sinister phrase, with the feminine posses-
sive, have been applied to the female slave.
Even Victorian England could not think long
about bought negresses without reflecting on
tell-tale shades receding from black, and
without visualising quadroons and octeroons
—yea, even, in a final distressing phantasy,
the wrong kind of president's daughters !

Among those who, on the public platform, exposed the degradation of fatherhood associated with the slave-owners' production of human hybrids, was Newman Hall, the famous Congregational minister, who was visited on October 19th, 1863, by a fugitive slave whose father had been her master and torturer, who had employed her to suckle his other children, and who had sold her own child into slavery.

The visits of fugitive slaves were, in fact, important factors in forming the passion which raged against " the South " in the American Civil War from British platforms.

On Saturday, November 30th, 1861, my father writes in his diary :—

" Mr. Matthews brought William Waterman ' a contraband,' who took the liberty of relieving his master of all further responsibility in relation to him in July last . . . He literally walked penniless and shoeless through the States of [word illegible] Maryland, Pennsylvania and New York until he arrived in Western Canada. A few people here and there assisted him with money, food and clothing. From Western Canada he begged his way to Quebec, where he took passage for Liverpool as steward on board of a merchant vessel. He gave entire satisfaction to the captain, who wrote him a special certificate of character . . . Gave him ten shillings on behalf of the [Emancipation] Committee."

On November 7th, 1862, my father writes :—

" Saw ' Jeff Davis's coachman,' who has just arrived. Jackson is literally the runaway coachman of the Confederate President. He is a black, sprightly, young-looking man."

On the 9th the diarist resumes :—

" At Mr. [George] Thompson's in evening. Talking to Jeff Davis's coachman. He drove out Mrs. Jefferson Davis, a fine, handsome, pretty woman. Davis is treated with no more personal respect than any other citizen. He said a very good thing about [Major-General G. B.] McClellan—that ' he was a very able General, but slow, as he always gave them plenty of time to keep out of the way.' "

It is true that Russia and Austria were both figuring as brutal tyrants at the time to which we are looking back, and true also is it that amongst ourselves was a savagery equal to the acts and defence of a Governor Eyre, who was not a monster, but a type. Still nominal slavery was the most real slavery, and its odour travelled, willy-nilly, across the Atlantic, and was not admired.

Hence, after the formation, on May 28th, 1859, in my father's Bloomsbury residence (19 Harpur Street), of the London Emancipation Committee, there arose, on November 11th, 1862, the Emancipation Society, whose offices were 65 Fleet Street, London. One of its founders, if not its originator, was Samuel Lucas, managing proprietor of *The Morning Star*, who presided over its first meeting and was the first subscriber to its funds. Mr. William Evans was chairman, Messrs. P. A. Taylor, M.P., and W. T. Malleson were joint treasurers, and my father, F. W. Chesson, was honorary secretary. At their offices were sold Professor John Elliott Cairnes's *The Revolution in America*, Tom Hughes's *The Cause of Freedom*, and other tracts. There was also the Ladies' Emancipation Society, which met on one occasion or more at Mrs. P. A. Taylor's house at Notting Hill, London.

The Union and Emancipation Society of Manchester, whose president was the eminent Free Trader, T. B. Potter, and whose secretaries were Mr. John C. Edwards and my friend, the eminent agriculturist, Mr. Edward Owen Greening, issued what I suppose was its first circular in April 1863. Mr. T. B. Potter informed my father on the 27th of that April that " he had spent between three to four thousand pounds on the Manchester Emancipation Movement." [1] Among inter-

---

[1] See page 107 for what it cost him altogether.

esting expressions of opinion evoked in 1863 by Mr. Potter in corresponding for this Society I select the following :—

W. E. Forster, writing on March 3rd, declined the vice-presidency, thinking he could serve " our common cause, viz. the promotion of Emancipation, better both in the House and out of it by not giving you my name."

Peter Rylands, writing on the 16th of March :—

" Cannot be a party in supporting the War Measures of the Northern Government. I hold that it is never right to do evil that good may come. War is an enormous evil, and the fratricidal war now being ruthlessly carried on in the States must be disastrous in its consequences to the whole world. I will neither directly nor indirectly be an abettor of it . . . I have a strong opinion that when the history of this struggle is written in after times the course pursued by the Northern Government will be judged to be very similar to that adopted by the Government of George the Third in attempting to put down by bloodshed the rebellion of the American colonies."

James Martineau wrote on March 20th :—

" In the interests of Emancipation itself, I

am driven to quite different political conclu-
sions from those on which the new Society is
based."

The Duke of Argyll (Lord Privy Seal), on
March 25th, wrote that :—

" It would be obviously improper for me as
a member of the Government to have charge
of the Petition you have sent to me.   I could
only present it in silence.   I therefore return
it that you may select some Peer who, if he
thinks right, can draw attention to its prayer."

On March 30th, the Archbishop of York
(Dr. William Thomson) wrote :—

" I wish I were able to sympathise with the
sentiments put forth by so many good and
able men.   The emancipation of all slaves and
the speedy termination of a bloody and waste-
ful war are indeed objects to be desired and
prayed for, by me as by you.   But in my
humble judgment these objects will not be
attained through the restoration of the Union
in America."

Prof. Thorold Rogers wrote on April 14th :—

" Every one who believes in the benefits of
popular government and hopes for the progress
of mankind in that habit of obedience to law
and order which always forms the basis of all
popular institutions, must feel the strongest

repugnance to the principle on which the seceded States attempted to commence their political existence, and the dishonourable means they adopted to carry out their projects."

Charles Kingsley wrote to Mr. Potter on March 21st :—

" With all respect for the good intentions of ' Arbitration ' and ' Emancipation ' Societies, I have satisfied myself, after intimate and long study—commencing with boyhood —of the Negro Question, that I cannot help the prospects of that unhappy Race by joining any such society; but that I may very probably help to injure them."

Apropos Kingsley's "long study," Mr. Arthur B. Potter, son of the President of the Union and Emancipation Society, adds an interesting sequel to the above letter or to an even franker assertion of dissentient opinion on the part of this "muscular Christian."

" Some time after the Civil War was over," he writes, " my father was sitting one night in the Century Club, talking to some one (it was Fawcett, I believe), when he felt a touch on his shoulder. Looking up, he saw Kingsley, who said, ' Mr. Potter, allow me to interrupt

you for just one minute. With regard to the
American Civil War, you were right and I was
wrong. That's all. Good-night.' "
Bravo, Kingsley !

The magnificent veteran, Baron Brougham
and Vaux, whose phrase about slavery—" the
wild and guilty phantasy that man can hold
property in man "—is perhaps as well known
as any definition of a public sin, was not
always, during the Civil War, an orator to the
liking of friends of freedom and the North.
On Thursday, June 5th, 1862, my father
diarises thus about Lord Brougham's speech
at the sixth annual meeting of the National
Association for the Promotion of Social
Science :—

" Lord Brougham begins to look very old
[he was born September 19th, 1778] and to
exhibit all the signs of decay. Probably not
more than 100 people heard a dozen con-
secutive sentences, so feeble was his voice.
He, however, threw some energy into his
tirade against democracy and his denuncia-
tion of America, which were in very bad
taste."

In *The Times* report of Lord Brougham's
speech he says :—

" In all ages the tendency of democratic rule has been to promote war, while aristocratic States, from Sparta downwards, have been fond of peace. But the conduct of the operations of war, as well as engaging in that evil course, is to a great degree in the hands of the multitude, when their voice prevails in the counsels of the State; that is to say, those who are wholly ignorant and unfit to advise are predominant over the skilful and well-informed."

Lord Brougham, however, paid a handsome compliment to the Northern Government for agreeing " to the mutual right of search (of suspected ships), in other words, to abolish all that remains of the Slave Trade."

The " prudent reserve " of Jefferson Davis, President of the Southern Republic of rebels against the Union, enables controversy to rage about the cause of the Civil War; and the effect to be looked for if the South had won was so hidden from the view even of the observatory in Printing-House Square that, on January 29th, 1863, it was possible for the forthright author of *Tom Brown's School Days* to speak as follows at a meeting convened by the Emancipation Society. I quote from *The Times* report :—

" Mr. Thomas Hughes said the question which was daily becoming more distinctly visible in connection with the contest in America was which is the side of freedom? That question had been answered lately on behalf of the British people by *The Times* [hisses]. . . . It stated that Englishmen were deeply impressed with the conviction that the cause in which the South was gallantly defending itself against the cruel and desolating invasion of the North was the cause of freedom [hisses]. . . . He was there to contend that the cause of the South was the cause not of freedom, but of the most degrading and hateful slavery which the world had seen for a thousand years."

It was at the same meeting (January 29th, 1863) that

" Mr. Matthew Field claimed the right to move an amendment characterising the emancipation proclamation as unconstitutional, vindictive, and diabolical, and affirming that the recognition of Southern independence would ultimately secure freedom to the negro. This amendment was received with a perfect tumult of groans and hisses, and its proposer was obliged to abandon the attempt to finish his speech, which he read from a manuscript half-concealed by his hat."

The Matthew Fields might say what they

liked, and journalists and politicians might reduce the quarrel of the Civil Warriors to an affair of Pot *versus* Kettle, but there were many fine minds in Great Britain which regarded the American Civil War as essentially a struggle between the friends of freedom and the profiteers of slavery.

George Thompson, in his speech at Leeds, March 25th, 1862, powerfully exhibited the slavery-bias as the diabolic inspiration of the South, quoting Preston Brooks of South Carolina, " the man who made the brutal and cowardly attack upon Mr. Charles Sumner." Brooks had said at the banquet which rewarded his assault, " If I was the commander of an army, I would not post a sentinel until he had sworn that slavery was right." Thompson quoted also Senator Brown of Mississippi, who said, with a candour defying parody, " I want Cuba, I want Tamaulipas, Potosí, and one or two other Mexican States, and I want them all for the same reason—for the planting and spreading of slavery. I would spread the blessings of slavery as I would spread the religion of our Divine Master, to the uttermost ends of the earth; and libellous and wicked as the Yankees have been, I would extend the blessings of slavery even to them."

In finishing his review of Southern oratory
Thompson remarked, " In these speeches you
find no allusion to higher tariffs or Federal
taxation, or to anything but the institution
of negro slavery."

John Bright, in a letter to my father dated
January 14th, 1864, defined the American
Civil War as " a desperate war intended by
the slave-owners to make slavery perpetual."
John Stuart Mill in his *Autobiography* (1873)
states that :—

" Having been a deeply interested observer
of the slavery quarrel in America during the
many years that preceded the open breach,
I knew that it was in all its stages an aggressive enterprise of the slave-owners to extend
the territory of slavery, under the combined
influences of pecuniary interest, domineering
temper, and the fanaticism of a class for its
class privileges."

If Jefferson Davis was reserved, it is true
that statesmanship and steering were the
cause of Lincoln's appearing as a far from
ideal leader from the viewpoint of those whose
eyes impatiently turned to him from an
unattained goal. With a shout of " Lincoln's
been and gone and done it ! " a friend of my

mother communicated to her on October 4th, 1862, what my father called "the glorious news" of Lincoln's Proclamation (September 22nd, 1862) of Emancipation, and this shout was like a pæan for relieved anxiety.

The poetic tribute in *Punch* to the assassinated Lincoln is well known, but ink does not expunge ink, and the anti-Lincolnism of the hunchback of St. Bride is not ignored by students of life. Thus, under a picture of crinolines and young ladies playing croquet, we listen to Abe (the American President) saying to the Russian Tsar Alexander in October 1863 :—

> " Bound to this child in bloody sympathies,
> Come to my arms, and let us be allies !
> We'll squelch JOHN BULL, and scuttle Britain's isle ;
> But let us go and liquor up meanwhile."

A less homely rhymer in the same number of *Punch* where the above appears, detesting the *rapprochement* between the Transatlantic Republic and the oppressor of Poland, sings of " Columbia's " flag that :—

> " Its *stripes* full well may fraternise
> With Russia's knout that women scars,
> But while it waves o'er such allies,
> Blot, oh, blot out, the indignant *stars !*"

That " the indignant stars " had tolerated

slavery with all its abominations compels the critic to view them on that occasion as mere asterisks, but it is fair to record that *Punch* did not believe in the philanthropy of the North.

"An afterthought only is ' Justice to Niggers,' "

he remarks in a clever address of " Britisher to Beecher," whom Tenniel figured as attempting to administer brimstone and treacle to the British Lion.

That disparaging criticism of Lincoln during the Civil War proceeded from a thoughtful consideration of his attitude and actions by really humane people is easily demonstrated.

A genius of scholarship and sincerity, John William Colenso, Bishop of Natal, wrote to Mr. T. B. Potter on April 10th, 1863 :—

" I need hardly say that I think it a monstrous iniquity to hold in fetters the bodies and souls of men. But the horrible letter of President Lincoln, in which he said that he would maintain slavery wholly or partially, if that would help him to maintain the Union, makes me very distrustful of the spirit which really animates the governing party of the Northern States. And I am by no means sure that the most helpful results for the slave are not rather to be looked for from an appeal to the Southern States themselves. . . . I would rather decline, under present circumstances, the honour of being a Vice-President of the Emancipation Society."

My father writes in his diary under June 27th, 1863 :—

" In afternoon Henry Ward Beecher came to the office. He is a fine specimen of an American—frank, genial, witty, and a good talker. Mr. Lincoln he described as a good, honest, well-meaning, stupid man—' a crab.' He [Lincoln] is a long time making up his mind, but when it is made up he sticks to his opinion even through failure and disaster."

On June 14th, 1864, Prof. F. W. Newman wrote to F. W. Chesson :—

" Lincoln was elected *to forbid the area of slavery from extending, and to maintain the principle that slavery was local, not national.* The terms of the former were stringent and he has been faithful to it. The latter was *not* formulated *strictly enough,* and he has become the victim of Southern influence. He has thrown overboard the Republican interpretation of the Constitution, and admitted that slavery is a national institution, which he is bound to sustain even in a State which has rebelled, and from which he is relieved only in the crisis of impending total ruin.

Evidently nothing can bind him but the
strictest lawyer-like bond. He obeys the
letter against moral principle; and almost
boasts of it. The work to be done proved,
in a few months after his election, to be totally
different from the work which he was elected
to do. Trial has abundantly shown that
he does it unwillingly, badly, at enormous
expense, and with imminent risk of ultimate
failure. Wendell Phillips remarks that the
President took but two months or so to abolish
habeas corpus, and near two years to consent
to freeing one slave of rebels. What possible
reply is there? Mr. Seward, you have probably seen, propounds that ' he loves his
country more than white freedom or than
black freedom.' What is this but to prepare
one for treachery? . . . I never believed the
imputations on Seward until now."

On November 3rd, 1864, Prof. Newman
writes to my father that he " was assured
by an accurate person . . . that Mr. Seward
said to him some years ago, ' We hate slavery;
but we hate the coloured race still more.' "

In connection with Prof. Newman's distrust
of Lincoln, a quotation from a " special
minute " prepared by F. W. Chesson for the
Emancipation Society, and unanimously
adopted by them on June 20th, 1864, is
apropos :—

" They [the Committee of the E. S.] have seen with deep regret that General [Nathaniel Prentiss] Banks's ordinances establishing a system of serfdom in the State of Louisiana have apparently been sanctioned by the authorities at Washington. These ordinances, embodying as they do the very principle of slavery, that of the right of the white man to coerce the black, may, if unrepealed, prepare the way for the complete re-establishment of the institution even in the districts where it is supposed to be virtually overthrown."

Nevertheless, there is no doubt that Lincoln detested slavery ever after seeing " a fine mulatto girl pinched, prodded, and trotted up and down " an auction-room at New Orleans. John Banks heard him say, " If ever I get a chance to hit that thing [slavery] I will hit it hard " (*see* the Hon. Ralph Shirley's convenient and interesting *Short Life of President Lincoln* (1919)).

My father's diary records on April 26th, 1865, that he was " horror-struck to-day by the news of President Lincoln's assassination," an event which deprived the world of this great man on the 15th of that month.

This delayed "horror" reminds us that the Atlantic Cable, which W. H. Seward said would remove the danger of misunderstanding between England and the U.S.A., was not yet operating, though from July 27th, 1866, England has thereby conversed with America so conveniently that, by the playful benevolence of latitude and longitude, our messages have an air of arriving before they are sent.

We obtain an amusing glimpse of the difficulties of a topical orator in England during the American Civil War in the following letter, written by George Thompson to his son-in-law, F. W. Chesson, from Portsea, on October 13th, 1863 :—

"I had a large, crowded and enthusiastic gathering in the Victorian Rooms, Ryde, last night, where I lectured for the Ryde Young Men's Christian Association. They had obtained as chairman on the occasion the Rev. Boys Smith, a popular Low Church clergyman—a pert, pragmatical, self-sufficient person, who is, notwithstanding, I daresay, a very good man. Taking me aside, he gave me a lecture in the way in which I should treat my subject. I must not be political; I must not go into the *causes* of the war; I must not allude to the conduct of the British

Government; I must not express a preference for North or South; I must not advocate immediate emancipation; I must not marshal my facts so as to make them tell more for one side than the other, etc., etc.

"Not content with lecturing me in private, he repeated the dose when he delivered his opening address, which he concluded by saying that he believed the feelings of the great majority of our countrymen were with the South.

"This was too much, so for two hours and a half I earnestly devoted myself to his instruction in truth and righteousness; and if not to his pleasure and profit, at least to the edification and delight of a great and respectable meeting, most of whom heard for the first time an exposition of the merits of the question. Nevertheless, I kept within the limits prescribed by the rules of the Association. At the conclusion of my address I was invited to come again, and in the same place, but upon a *free* platform, to pour out all I had to say upon every branch of the subject."

The brilliant Washington Wilks, whose sudden death on a public platform occurred on June 28th, 1864, eulogised George Thompson in 1863 as one "who traversed the length and breadth of the land striking down every fallacy which has been raised in favour

of the South with a power of logic, a keen-
ness of sarcasm and an extent of information
upon the subject unequalled by any other
man."

Touching Wilks's own good work in forming right opinion about the American Civil
War, the following extract from my father's
diary on November 5th, 1863, is of interest :—

" Attended Wilks's lecture in evening on
' Pro-Southern Englishmen.' He hit off Beres-
ford Hope [one of the founders of *The
Saturday Review*], [John Arthur] Roebuck
[M.P. for Sheffield], [William Schaw] Lindsay
[M.P. for Sunderland], and [Charles] Mackay
[poet and special correspondent of the London
Times at New York during the Civil War], to
the life."

On the 25th of the same November Wilks
and my father attended an Emancipation
Meeting at Greenwich, where the proceedings
included " a fight on the platform."   " However, we carried our resolution," says my
diarist.

Henry Ward Beecher's oratorical tour in
Great Britain in 1863 had in Scotland the
distinction of a combat against clamour.
The son of Bailie Govan, who took the chair

in the meeting held at the City Hall, Glasgow, on October 13th, 1863, relates that on that occasion "Beecher and his Chairman stood together" for a full quarter of an hour facing a turbulent sea of noisy hostility. "At an opportune moment Beecher managed to utter one sentence : "I am proud to stand in the country of the man who wrote 'a man's a man for a' that.'" That sentence, according to Mr. Arthur Govan, enabled Beecher to hold his audience until he had poured into it his "torrent of fiery and convincing eloquence."

This incident is overlooked in the compilation called *American Rebellion*, which contains the reports of Beecher's speeches in Manchester, Glasgow, Edinburgh, Liverpool and London in 1863. At Liverpool Beecher's chairman deemed it wise to mention the police as an available instrument for dealing with "disorderly conduct," but Beecher was one of those whose oratory accepts hostility as aliment. We even find him asking his admirers to restrain their enthusiasm : "You will observe," he informs them on the Liverpool night of October 16, 1863, "that my voice is slightly husky from having spoken almost every night in succession for some time past. Those who wish to hear me

will do me the kindness simply to sit still
and to keep still; and I and my friends the
Secessionists will make all the noise." After
"interruption and uproar" he remarks:
"There is luck in leisure; I'm going to take
it easy." The humour and eloquence of a
Beecher could make their mark in any
popular controversy. When, at Manchester,
he had told his hearers that the profitableness
of cotton after the invention of the cotton
gin had stopped the "onward tide" of
emancipation, he said :—

"Slaves that before had been worth from
300 to 400 dollars, began to be worth 600
dollars. That knocked away one-third of
adherence to the moral law. Then they
became worth 700 dollars, and half the law
went; then 800 or 900 dollars, and then
there was no such thing as moral law; then
1000 or 1200 dollars, and slavery became one
of the beatitudes."

Exeter Hall—that factory of reformation
whose function is to-day fulfilled by the
Albert Hall—was the scene of one of Beecher's
great speeches on October 20th, 1863. My
father writes that the hall was then " crammed
to overflowing,

" and thousands were outside clamouring in

vain for admission. Mr. Beecher had great difficulty in getting in, and when he mounted the platform he was received with a perfect hurricane of applause. His speech was a splendid effort, and was followed by my resolution [of thanks to Beecher and sympathy " with his reprobation of the slaveholders' rebellion "], moved by Prof. Newman, seconded by Newman Hall, and supported by George Thompson."

Beecher was to *Punch* merely a professional doing his job for greenbacks. However, a minute book in my library informs me that at a meeting of the Executive Committee, held at the offices of the Emancipation Society on November 2nd, 1863, Mr. Edmond Beales being in the chair, it was " resolved that this Committee hereby records its high sense of the invaluable services rendered to the cause of Negro Emancipation and of international peace by the Rev. H. W. Beecher during his visit to this country . . ." and it was also resolved that " the foregoing resolution, together with the one adopted at the meeting at Exeter Hall, be neatly engraved on vellum and transmitted to the Rev. H. W. Beecher at New York."

The part played by Charles Dickens in

conveying the United States of 1842 in truthful satire to England is well known to readers of *Martin Chuzzlewit*. In a letter to Mrs. Henry Austin (November 7th, 1862), he refers to Napoleon III's earnest proposal for a Franco-Russo-British appeal to stop " the brutal war," but he adds, " I think I clearly perceive that the proposal will be declined." In his *All the Year Round* for December 28th, 1861, Dickens printed an article called " The Morrill Tariff," in which an anonymous writer states " that the quarrel between North and South is, as it stands, solely a fiscal quarrel."

In 1865, when the *Alabama*, whose naughtiness cost great Britain 15½ million dollars as a result of the Treaty of Washington (1871), had, as a controversial subject, displaced a quantity of ink almost sufficient to have floated her as a piratical object, Dickens wrote (November 13th) to M. De Cerjat :—

" If the Americans don't embroil us in a war before long it will not be their fault. What with their swagger and bombast, what with their claims for indemnification, what with Ireland and Fenianism, and what with Canada, I have strong apprehensions. With a settled animosity towards the French usurper [Napoleon III] I believe him to have always been sound in his desire to divide the States against themselves, and that we were unsound and wrong in 'letting I dare not wait upon I would.' That Jamaica insurrection is another hopeful piece of business. That platform-sympathy with the black—or the native, or the devil—afar off, and that platform-indifference to our own countrymen at enormous odds in the midst of bloodshed and savagery, make me stark wild."

"Stark wild" is just; nothing is less creditable to human intelligence than the fact that ease in communication begets slipsloppy thought. In real life the spectacle of an Eyre suppressing a rising would have infuriated Dickens, and he who described the reign of Henry VIII as "a drop of blood and grease on the history of England," would have been fortunate in escaping a rhetorical apoplexy if he had been able to peep at nineteenth-century slave life in South Carolina and Georgia.

In his pamphlet, *The Relations between America and England* (1869), Goldwin Smith remarks that Bright's speech at St. James's Hall, London, on March 26th, 1863,

is " the greatest of all his speeches."   Bright,
who, my father says, " was troubled with
hoarseness and had to speak in very measured
tones," spoke then to " a meeting composed
of artisans and working-men of the city of
London "—the Trades Unions, in fact.   It is
a speech which reminds us of his sobriquet
"the great Tribune."   He summoned up
Privilege as a bodily presence; he reminded
his audience " that a loan has been con-
tracted for in the City to the amount of three
millions sterling, on behalf of the Southern
Confederacy "—" to pay in this country for
. . . . *Alabamas*."   He told them that

" there are men sitting amongst your legis-
lators who will build and equip corsair ships
to prey upon the commerce of a friendly
power; who will disregard the laws and the
honour of their country ; who will trample on
the Proclamation of their sovereign, and
who, for the sake of the glittering profit
which sometimes waits on crime, are content
to cover themselves with everlasting infamy."

Lord Denison wrote on March 24th, 1863,
to Mr. Potter :—

" Another British slave ship of war has
gone to sea . . .
" The bribe of the American slaveholders'

rebellion is taken in London, in part by British merchants, to the amount of three millions of pounds, at the rate of four per cent. per annum.

"We must prepare for war between England and America and the enfranchisement of the British people.

"Are you ready?"

In his *Reminiscences* (1899), Justin McCarthy recalls that :—

"When the Civil War in the United States broke out, and nine out of every ten men in what was called London society, and in the House of Commons itself, were firmly convinced that the Southern Confederation was certain to hold its own and establish its independence, if, indeed, it did not occupy Washington and set up its own President there, Mr. Cobden quietly smiled at the ignorance of those who took such dreamings for realities, and gave his own reasons, drawn from his own personal knowledge, for holding the opinions which time afterwards proved to be right."

In a letter written from Algiers, March 20th, 1861, to Mr. Thomas Balch, an American who was deeply interested in the preservation of peace between America and England, Cob-

den sees no reason why " separation of North
and South " should be " resisted on either
side. So that it be done peaceably," he
proceeds—

" I don't see why separate governments
might not present a better chance of good
neighbourhood than compulsory Union. I
am sorry to see Congress taking a retrograde
step on the tariff. They will, however, soon
find that ' protection ' is inconsistent with a
flourishing revenue or a prosperous trade,
and then they will retrace their steps. Meantime your countrymen are giving too much
ground to the enemies of Republicanism for
disparaging the wisdom and virtues of
democracy ! "

Cobden disapproved of the North's blockade (*vide* John Bright's correspondence with
Charles Sumner) ; but Mrs. Cobden (his widow)
was assured, in a letter dated May 15th,
1865, by a friend of Lincoln that Lincoln
always spoke of Cobden " in the same spirit
of kindliness and affection ; and only a week
before Mr. Cobden's death I was in receipt
of a letter from our great orator, Wendell
Phillips, who expressed his sincere gratification in the fact that your husband had spoken
of his esteem for him. . . ."

The death of Richard Cobden on April 2nd, 1865, grief for which is said to have shortened the life of Samuel Lucas, who died a fortnight after him (on the 16th), also greatly shocked my father, who, in all his migrations, never allowed the second-hand bookseller to acquire a copy of " Speeches of Richard Cobden . . . delivered during 1849," which that orator presented to him on June 21st, 1852. " Mr. Cobden spoke, as he always does, with infinite clearness and good sense," writes my father in his diary for June 19th, 1862 ; and this was not the remark of an habitual hyperbolist—quite the reverse.

A striking anecdote with regard to the bye-election necessitated by Cobden's death is told by Mr. Arthur B. Potter.

" My father," he says, " stood for Rochdale in the spring of 1865 against Brett (afterwards Lord Esher). . . . It was before the Ballot Act, and in those days the state of the poll was published from hour to hour, and the excitement was very great. When the result was announced, my father had to make a speech to the huge crowd gathered together in the Square. He thanked the people for returning him, and said that the result would be good news for their friends in London. Then he added, ' But I have better

news for you.' Immediately there was a
dead silence, the crowd not being able to
understand what he referred to. 'Richmond has fallen.' Then arose a cheer louder
and more deafening than any of the previous.
Dayton, the son of the American Minister at
Paris, who had come to Rochdale to see what
an English election was like, had been
standing behind my father, and he said,
'Mr. Potter, if that cheer could have been
carried across the Atlantic, Americans would
think very differently of your country.'"

I am late in mentioning the revered Queen
Victoria, but would here say that her writings
show her to have been nobly sensitive to
slights which, if too indiscriminately tolerated,
disgrace neutrality. Thus, respecting "the
forcible capture of the Southern Envoys
from on board the *Trent* steamer," which
Viscount Palmerston's Cabinet regarded, to
quote his letter of November 29th, 1861,
as "a gross outrage and violation of international law," the Queen remarked that she
would have liked to have seen in the British
Government's draft of a dispatch to the
American Government

"the expression of a hope that the American
captain did not act under instructions, or, if

he did, that he misapprehended them—that the United States Government must be fully aware that the British Government could not allow its flag to be insulted, and the security of her mail communications to be placed in jeopardy. . . ."

On December 14th, 1861, the Prince Consort died, and the Queen described to Earl Canning her state of mind in bereavement as " death in life," with " the whole nation to look to her—*now*, when she can barely struggle with her wretched existence ! " (And among those who " looked to her " was " Pam " himself, altruistically wishing her to confer baronetcies on three individuals, one of whom was recommended for the honour as being " a rich and highly respectable gentleman of the county of Carnarvon.")

By the way, on October 18th, 1865, my father writes :—

" Lord Palmerston died at a quarter to eleven o'clock this morning. We sent Kendall down to Brocket Hall [on the Lea, Hertfordshire]. He found that it was not intended to publish the news in the evening papers, but after seeing one of the physicians and Lord Shaftesbury (who was weeping) he got the news and telegraphed it in time for the second edition. The servant whom he first saw had the hardihood to tell him that Lord Palmerston was much better, although he had been dead three hours."

Pam, "the wonderful old man," as my father elsewhere calls him, was not insensible to the humour of American relations at the dinner-table, and related how on one occasion the Haytian Ambassador sat "between the American and Brazilian Ministers."

In drawing to a close, I find myself in contact again with the historian and publicist, Professor Goldwin Smith. Smith said to his bright Boswell (Mr. Arnold Haultain) on the Day of Independence, 1898, "I do not believe in the 'categorical imperative' or what-not. There is no such thing as Right or Wrong." By these words one might imagine him as a species of super-terrestrial eye and ear insensitive to suffering and iniquity. His life shows him, however, to have been well aware of the difference between happy and unhappy humanity. In his old age he dubbed Swinburne a "raving, ranting person," but it was not because he was himself incapable of the rhapsody of the rhetorician inspired by the large jubilance of a victorious cause. There is some-

thing of the majesty of Flaubert in that
passage of his address, " The Civil War in
America," delivered on January 22nd, 1866,
where he says :—

" Not the fields on which Greek intellect
and art were saved from the Persian; not
the fields on which Roman law and polity
were saved from the Carthaginian and the
Gaul; not those plains of Tours on which
Charles Martel rolled back Islam from the
heart of Christendom; not the waters over
which the shattered Armada fled; not Leip-
sic and Lutzen, Marston and Naseby, where,
at the hands of Gustavus and Cromwell, the
great reaction of the seventeenth century
found its doom, will be so consecrated by
the gratitude of after ages as Vicksburg and
Gettysburg, Atlanta and those lines before
Richmond which saw the final blow."

After this outburst one is amused by the
very different tone discernible in our " high
politics " when the blessed event which inspired Goldwin Smith was like a great flower
newly crowning a thorny stem. On Saturday, July 1st, 1865, my father writes in his
diary :—

" In afternoon went up with deputation to
Lord Russell [Secretary of State] to ask him

to insert a paragraph in the Queen's speech expressing gratification with the abolition of slavery in America. Kept waiting an hour and a quarter, Lord Russell being at a Cabinet Council. He said that the Cabinet were opposed to the mention of the subject in that way. He was more amiable than usual."

Unfortunately, on returning to Goldwin Smith's " address," after chilling ourselves with Earl Russell's amiability, we find that rhetoric ran away with the Professor, for in his peroration he said : " Be these the last words of the Association which ends its course to-night, SLAVERY IS DÉAD EVERY-WHERE AND FOR EVER." True it was that on that night, namely, January 22nd, 1866, the Union Emancipation Society ceased to exist, but even when the century had changed its name, the crimes against liberty in the Congo and at Putamayo taxed the energy of a Society which still has grave cause for existence and support, though its name continues to be The Anti-Slavery and Aborigines' Protection Society.

But irony should not dictate the last words of a book like this. In the decree of

emancipation, whether it was or was not
"an afterthought" on the part of an individual statesman, the immortal life in the
noble purpose of an indomitable though
persecuted minority was made manifest;
and with the extinction of American slavery
the harmony between Britons and Americans
ceased to depend upon the suppression of a
loathing for a horrible injustice. Never—not
even in the Venezuelan crisis of December 1895
—have the two great Anglo-Saxon nations
been so nearly in the arena of Mars as in the
days of wholesale fratricide when one out of
every twenty-six Americans was a soldier.
While it may be that eagles and unicorns are
still fit emblems for the patriotic energy of
many people, the ruling minds of the world
are not what they were. The minority that
works for the Federation of Mankind has
ceased to be regarded as a congregation of
dreamers, and it is not rash to hope that
Anglo-American Relations may remain "un-
sensational" too long for the historian of the
future to deem it profitable to write new
chapters on this theme.